PENGUIN  CLASSICS

# PROTAGORAS AND MENO

PLATO stands, with his teacher Socrates and his pupil Aristotle, as one of the shapers of the entire intellectual tradition of the West. Born *c.* 427 BC, he came from a family that had long played a prominent part in Athenian politics, and it would have been natural for him to follow the same course; the reason for his not doing so, according to the seventh of the collection of letters attributed to him (all of them almost certainly inauthentic), was his disillusionment with the kind of politics that could lead, among other things, to the execution – in 399 – of Socrates. Rather less plausibly, the same letter suggests that Plato's several visits to the court of Dionysius II, tyrant of Syracuse in Sicily, were motivated by a desire to put his political theories – as developed above all in his masterwork, *Republic* – into practice. The reform of society on an ethical basis certainly remained one of his central theoretical concerns. However, the focus of his thinking was on ethics itself, in which he first followed and then went beyond Socrates, and on metaphysics and the understanding of reality. In the mid-380s, in Athens, he founded the Academy, the first permanent institution devoted to philosophical research and teaching, and an institution to which all Western universities like to trace their origins.

Plato wrote more than twenty philosophical dialogues, appearing in none himself (most have Socrates as chief speaker). His activity as a writer seems to have lasted over half a century; few authors in any language could claim to rival his particular combination of brilliant artistry and intellectual power. He died in 347 BC.

ADAM BERESFORD studied Classics at Balliol College, Oxford. He taught Latin and Greek at Dulwich College, London, from 1993 to 1995, and received a doctorate in Philosophy from Oxford in 2002. He teaches Philosophy and Classics at the University of Massachusetts, Boston.

LESLEY BROWN is Centenary Fellow in Philosophy at Somerville College, Oxford, and the author of numerous articles and book chapters on Plato and Aristotle.

# PLATO

# Protagoras *and* Meno

*Translated by* ADAM BERESFORD
*with an Introduction by* LESLEY BROWN

PENGUIN BOOKS

PENGUIN CLASSICS

Published by the Penguin Group

Penguin Books Ltd, 80 Strand, London WC2R ORL, England

Penguin Group (USA) Inc., 375 Hudson Street, New York, New York 10014, USA

Penguin Group (Canada), 90 Eglinton Avenue East, Suite 700, Toronto, Ontario, Canada M4P 2Y3
(a division of Pearson Penguin Canada Inc.)

Penguin Ireland, 25 St Stephen's Green, Dublin 2, Ireland
(a division of Penguin Books Ltd)

Penguin Group (Australia), 250 Camberwell Road, Camberwell, Victoria 3124, Australia
(a division of Pearson Australia Group Pty Ltd)

Penguin Books India Pvt Ltd, 11 Community Centre, Panchsheel Park, New Delhi – 110 017, India

Penguin Group (NZ), cnr Airborne and Rosedale Roads, Albany, Auckland 1310, New Zealand
(a division of Pearson New Zealand Ltd)

Penguin Books (South Africa) (Pty) Ltd, 24 Sturdee Avenue, Rosebank, Johannesburg 2196, South Africa

Penguin Books Ltd, Registered Offices: 80 Strand, London WC2R ORL, England

www.penguin.com

This translation first published in 2005

025

Translation and editorial material © Adam Beresford, 2005
Introduction copyright © Lesley Brown, 2005
All rights reserved

The moral right of the translator has been asserted

Set in 10.25/12.25 pt PostScript Adobe Sabon
Typeset by Rowland Phototypesetting Ltd, Bury St Edmunds, Suffolk

Printed and bound in Great Britain by Clays Ltd, Elcograf S.p.A.

ISBN-13: 978-0-14-044903-7
ISBN-10 0-1404-903-5

www.greenpenguin.co.uk

# Contents

# Chronology

The rough idea we have of the chronology of Plato's life and career is partly based on guesses made from his own writings. For other details we rely on ancient biographies, all of them written over four hundred years after his death (which we hope are partly based on earlier sources) and on the letters attributed to him, which may or may not be genuine. Dates for the composition of the many dialogues that he wrote are speculative, but scholars broadly agree on whether a given work comes from earlier or later in his career, and that the dialogues may be divided roughly into three groups. *Protagoras* and *Meno* probably both date to the 380s BC, along with four other works that are similar in length and style and touch on many of the same themes: *Euthydemus*, *Symposium*, *Gorgias*, *Phaedo*. Together these make up a set that represents his most ambitious work as a dramatist and some of his most original and inventive philosophy. Also given here are a few dates that are relevant to the historical and dramatic settings of these particular dialogues.

c. 468 BC Birth of Socrates.

450s–430s Athens, as a flourishing democracy, under the leadership of Pericles, becomes the dominant power in the Aegean.

432 Dramatic date for the *Protagoras*. (It is set nearly fifty years before the date of its composition.)

431 Start of the Peloponnesian War (between Athens and Sparta).

430–429 Athens is hit by a catastrophic plague. Pericles dies.

c. 427 Birth of Plato, into a wealthy and aristocratic family.

c. 410s Plato first comes under the influence of Socrates.

415 Athens suffers a heavy defeat in an over-ambitious naval expedition against Syracuse, in Sicily.

404 Athens is decisively defeated by Sparta; the democratic government is replaced by a dictatorial oligarchy – 'The Thirty Tyrants' – which includes two of Plato's close relatives, Critias and Charmides. (There is a tradition that Plato was invited to take part, and refused.) Within a few months there is a civil war, and the oligarchy is overthrown by the democratic faction, led by Thrasybulus and Anytus, among others. The democracy is restored.

402 (early) Dramatic date for the *Meno*.

402 Cyrus, ruler of Asia Minor, and brother of Artaxerxes, the Persian king, attempts to oust his brother. He leads a large expeditionary force into the heart of Persia, partly made up of Greek mercenaries, including Meno, who serves as a general.

401 Cyrus' expedition fails. Meno is captured and executed.

399 Socrates is prosecuted by Anytus and two others. The charges are that he 'doesn't believe in the gods of the city' (a charge which implies subversion of traditional moral values) and that he 'corrupts young people'. He is found guilty, in a public trial, by a jury of 500 Athenian citizens, and sentenced to death. Socrates' death may have prompted Plato to give up on the idea of entering political life, and devote himself fully to philosophy. It also seems to have given him a deep mistrust of democratic institutions.

389–388 Plato travels to Sicily and southern Italy, where he visits and is influenced by Pythagorean schools there. (Pythagoreans believed in reincarnation, and apparently combined an interest in mathematics and geometry with number mysticism.)

390s–380s Probable period for Plato's composition of *Socrates' Defence Speech (Apology)*, *Euthyphro*, *Crito*, *Charmides*, *Cratylus*, *Hippias Minor*, *Menexenus*, *Ion*, *Laches*, *Lysis*, *Protagoras*, *Euthydemus*, *Meno*, *Gorgias*, *Symposium* and *Phaedo*.

c. 387 Plato founds the 'Academy' in Athens, a kind of philosophical school and proto-university (so named after its loca-
tion in a grove sacred to Academos, just outside the city).

380s–370s Probable period for the composition of *Republic*,
*Phaedrus*, *Parmenides*, and *Theaetetus*.

367 Plato visits Sicily again, at the invitation of his former pupil
Dion, the uncle of Dionysius II, king of Syracuse. (Some
ancient biographers say that Plato and Dion planned to edu-
cate the young Dionysius, and turn him into a 'philosopher-
king' – and that the experiment was a dismal failure; also
that Plato returned to Syracuse in 361 and tried one more
time to influence Dionysius, with the same result.)

360s–350s Probable period for composition of *Sophist*, *Statesman*, *Timaeus*, *Critias*, and *Laws* (known to be Plato's final
work).

347 Plato dies.

# Introduction

Plato was born in Athens in 427 BC into a wealthy and politically prestigious family. Athens was then at the height of her power and wealth, buzzing with new intellectual and cultural movements, and attracting leading thinkers and artists from all over the Greek world. Twenty-three years later, Athens had suffered a final defeat in the long wars against Sparta and her allies, and in 399 BC, before Plato was thirty, the newly restored democracy tried and executed Socrates, whose teachings and mode of life had such a profound influence on Plato and his other followers. In their dramatic settings, these two dialogues span this critical period. The *Protagoras* is set in about 432 BC, in the golden age of Pericles on the eve of the war that swept it away; the *Meno* is set in 402 BC, just after Athens' final defeat, and foreshadows Socrates' imminent trial and death.

The charges against Socrates, then aged seventy, were that he corrupted the youth of Athens and that he did not worship the city's gods. According to Plato's *Apology*, his version of the speech Socrates gave in his own defence at his trial, he strenuously denied these charges. Though he apparently wrote nothing, he was a leading member of the intellectual circles of his day. The Socrates of Plato's dialogues – at least of these ones – is an affable, ironic and infuriating questioner. He always claims he knows nothing at all about the serious questions he raises; he treats the people he talks to as his equals, and as partners in the search, and constantly asks them for their opinions, usually to show that they are hopelessly confused. He believes in moral inquiry and self-examination, and in the unique power of dialogue and of reason to advance human understanding.

Socrates was not a professional teacher but offered his conversation free of charge. Plato's writings very often aim to set him apart from the class of professional experts known as *sophists*. These sophists, three of whom are portrayed in the *Protagoras*, were often influential political figures in their own cities. They made huge names for themselves, and great fortunes, giving displays of their intellectual prowess and new ideas all over Greece. Sophists competed for fame and influence, and charged large fees for instruction in the various kinds of expertise they claimed to impart – which might include literary criticism, geometry, astronomy, music or even grammar. They were opening up new intellectual areas, and challenging the traditional forms of knowledge, with theories such as Protagoras' relativism: the claim that man is the measure of all things. Some, including Protagoras, claimed they could teach young men to become good: what exactly this entailed was a subject of considerable debate and disagreement, and forms the theme of our two works. But it certainly involved teaching ambitious young men the skills needed to make waves and acquire political influence, especially the art of public speaking, in an era when being a fine orator was key to a successful political life. Whether the sophists offered anything more – and in particular whether, like Socrates, they offered any kind of ethical instruction – was a question that greatly interested Plato. He presents Protagoras (whom he treats with more respect than most) as claiming to be an expert on ethical matters – and the investigation of that claim forms a theme of the work.

Apart from the *Apology*, Plato's writings are all cast in the form of dialogues, most of them with Socrates as the main speaker. They were written after his execution, in part no doubt to champion and celebrate him as a brilliant thinker and as one for whom the philosophic way of life was a matter of the utmost moral seriousness. But the reader should not expect faithful representations of discussions and doctrines actually held by Socrates, tempting though it is to speculate as to whether he actually encountered Protagoras, what they discussed and whether Socrates really held the views we find him putting forward in these dialogues.

Plato is unsurpassed as an original thinker and writer, and the *Protagoras* and *Meno* are among the best introductions to his thought and writings. They are closely linked in subject matter, each exploring the question of being good: What is it? What is the relation of its parts (such as bravery, or respect for what's right, or wisdom) to being good as a whole? How can a person hope to become good? Can some form of teaching make us good? However, each dialogue exemplifies a different facet of Plato's literary skill. In the *Protagoras*, we have Socrates describing to an unnamed friend two meetings: a private one with a young would-be student of Protagoras, and another, public gathering at which Socrates enters into a debate with the great sophist, while other luminaries gather round, each showing off and trying to grab the limelight in the manner of intellectuals then and now. The device of making Socrates the narrator allows him some knowing comments on how his and others' remarks were delivered and received, and the whole narration is a sparkling tour-de-force. The *Meno*, on the other hand, is in straight dramatic form: Socrates and the young, self-centred Meno address each other directly, and Meno's changing attitudes – at first he is cocky and self-assured, then demoralized, and finally a reinvigorated if chastened co-inquirer – are presented directly in the exchanges between the two.

## The Protagoras

In the *Protagoras*, the main drama, the exchange between Socrates and Protagoras, is preceded by a brief but important prelude, a private discussion between Socrates and Hippocrates, who is so impatient for an introduction to the famous sophist that he wakes Socrates before dawn. What does the young man hope to learn from associating with Protagoras? Socrates shows him that he has a very limited grasp of what it is that he wants, and of what a sophist can do for him. But they set off to see Protagoras all the same. Their arrival is a scene lifted from Greek comedy: they are blocked at the door by a grumpy slave before gaining entry to the house of Callias (a young millionaire who likes to throw his money at sophists) and the assembly of intellectuals. There follows a description of the three 'professors'; Protagoras walking, flanked by his deferential followers; Hippias, seated and addressing his from on high; Prodicus, pontificating to his admirers while wrapped up in bed. Everyone gathers round to hear the discussion between Socrates and Protagoras, which centres on this question: What will Protagoras teach the young Hippocrates?

'The very day you start your tuition, you'll go home *better* than you were before' – but better at what? 'Good decision-making, in private and public affairs.' Being a good citizen, then, is what Protagoras professes to teach, but Socrates wonders if this is really teachable. After all, the democratic assembly at Athens recognizes experts in technical matters but none, apparently, in what it takes to be a good citizen. Everyone (not just a few 'experts') is allowed to have a say on civic and ethical matters.

Protagoras' reply – a 'display-speech' typical of sophists – opens with a myth, a 'Just-So' story about the origin of morality. He skilfully negotiates the traps Socrates has laid for him. To defend his own profession, he must argue that being good *is* teachable, but he also wants to support the democratic policy of allowing anyone to speak on civic matters. His solution: to claim that being good can be and indeed is taught, but that in a civilized society *everyone* learns it – through teaching. His 'story' tells how human beings missed out on being endowed with natural defences (such as wings, claws or a tough skin) but, as a thoughtful compensation, were given fire, and technical skill, by the god Thinxahead (Prometheus). However, these still were insufficient for humans to thrive and defend themselves against wild animals, because they couldn't co-operate and kept fighting *each other*. Only a further gift, direct from Zeus, saved humankind from destruction: the gift of *aidós* and *díkë*: a sense of right and wrong. Importantly, Zeus instructed his messenger Hermes to give this not just to a few people but to *everyone*; and this universal sense of right and wrong – the foundation of civil society – was to be our salvation.

Protagoras next underlines the story's meaning. Athenians

are correct to regard everyone as being good, to at least a minimal degree, not by nature but through teaching. So who teaches people how to be good? Everyone. Everyone who in civil society takes part in bringing up children – mothers, nurses and neighbours – because 'we benefit from people being good to one another' (327b). This socialization is both a product of, and a prerequisite for, civil society. Hence in the story it is represented as a *late* gift from Zeus, not one with which human beings were endowed from the start, but one they acquired only after a period of unsuccessful attempts to live in groups. The speech ends with an ingenious explanation of why the sons of good men don't turn out good themselves despite their fathers' efforts – evidently a topic of some currency, discussed also in the *Meno* as a stumbling-block for the view that you can be taught to be good. The speech is a brilliant presentation of an essentially common-sense view that equates being good with socially instilled decent behaviour. It proposes that the sense of right and wrong is necessarily widespread since it arises, ultimately, from an instinct for the mutual respect and co-operation needed for communal living. But this kind of being good – possessing a basic ethical sense and minimally decent behaviour – has little to do with what ambitious young men would pay Protagoras good money to learn from him, a problem the speech skirts over rather unconvincingly. Nor is it enough for Socrates, who aspires to something much more intellectually grounded and much less commonplace.

The middle section of the dialogue is puzzling. Socrates raises an issue discussed in other dialogues: whether the different ways of being good – that is, the various ethical qualities, such as bravery and moderation – are all at bottom *one and the same thing*. This is the idea, also known as 'the unity of the virtues', that Aristotle ascribes, as the claim that all ethical qualities are 'forms of knowledge', to Socrates in his *Nicomachean Ethics* (6.13). Protagoras, again defending a common-sense view, maintains that the parts of being good are more like the parts of the face (all parts of one thing but unlike each other), and that people can have one – say, bravery – but lack another –

say, a concern for what's right (329). Socrates defends the view that the parts of being good are one and the same by mounting three arguments before the interlude: that respect for what's right is the same as religiousness; that knowledge and good sense are the same (on the ground that each is the opposite of stupidity); and that respect for what's right can be equated with good sense, though their argument is left unfinished because Protagoras gets impatient and goes off on a tangent.

These arguments have evident flaws, some of which Protagoras is allowed to point out. It is not uncommon to find in Plato's works plainly weak arguments used in defence of claims which nonetheless seem to be intended to be considered as serious options – such as the claim that all the different parts of being good are really at bottom a matter of a certain kind of knowledge (a claim that is repeated in both the *Laches* and the *Meno*). Plato meant these writings to serve in part as an *invitation* to philosophy, one that forces us to think through and evaluate, for ourselves, the claims made and the arguments used in support of them.

Another half-comic, half-serious section allows Plato both to poke more fun at the assembled sophists – parodying the nit-picking of Prodicus' verbal distinctions and the jargon-laden pomposity of Hippias – and to make some serious points about how proper discussions should proceed. The assembled worthies eventually agree to Socrates' preference for question-and-answer over the professors' liking for grand speeches, but now it is Protagoras' turn to do the asking, and his chosen subject is the meaning of a song written by Simonides. More parody follows, this time by Socrates, of the sophistic style of literary criticism. He tells an absurd story about the Spartans being closet-philosophers and rounds off with the withering remark that bringing poets into a conversation is like hiring flute-girls – the lap-dancers of the day.

The last stretch of the dialogue sees Socrates trying to persuade Protagoras and the others that all the parts of being good, even bravery, are just a kind of knowledge. This upshot to their debate, as Socrates points out in the personified voice of their Ending, reverses their initial positions, because at the opening of the discussion it had been Socrates casting doubt on whether being good could be taught, and Protagoras insisting that it could. Now Socrates is the one who is committed to the view that people can be taught to be good, since every part of being good – even bravery – is a kind of knowledge, and he assumes, here as in the *Meno*, that all kinds of knowledge can be taught.

Two fundamental philosophical issues are introduced in the last stretch, ones that are still debated today. Socrates (apparently) begins to advocate a version of *hedonism* – the view that the only good thing in life is pleasure – and in the process denies that it is ever possible to do something you know is bad for you. That is, he denies there is such a thing as 'lacking self-control' (also known as *akrasia*, or 'weakness of will'). What, he asks, is the relation of pleasure to the good, of something being pleasurable to its being a good thing? Are they the same? And is it possible for a person to know what's good but fail to do it, and choose something less good instead? In these discussions, we find Socrates and Protagoras united. They both hold, against the widespread view, that knowledge is *all-powerful* and cannot ever be defeated by contrary desires or emotions – by desire for pleasure, or by fear, or by anger. Socrates undertakes to disprove the popular view and tries to show that the common excuse – 'I did something I knew was bad, because I couldn't resist the pleasure' – involves an absurdity. He gets all parties to agree that what's pleasurable and what's good are one and the same, and likewise what's painful and what's bad. Then, by a clever substitution argument, the excuse becomes 'I did something I knew was bad because I couldn't resist what's good,' or, with the reverse substitution (replacing 'bad' by 'painful'), 'I did what I knew was painful, because I couldn't resist the pleasure.' Each of these statements is meant to sound self-evidently absurd.

The common view, then, that we sometimes knowingly choose the worse option must be replaced by Socrates' new diagnosis: what people call 'doing what you know is bad because you can't resist the pleasure' must in fact just be a matter of ignorance – i.e. of *not really knowing* that what you're doing is bad for you. Really – he insists – it's just a failure to *measure correctly* the pros and cons of alternative courses of action that accounts for such behaviour. This is the famous Socratic intellectualism. It assumes that a person's motivation must always reflect how they evaluate the alternatives and infers that a wrong choice must always flow from a wrong evaluation, never from succumbing to temptation in spite of *knowing* what is best (which most of us believe can happen pretty often). A closely related theme is presented much more briefly in the *Meno* at 77–8, where Socrates argues against Meno's idea that people can want something even though they *know* it is bad for them and harms them. If you agree with Meno, and with the 'ordinary people' who appear in the *Protagoras*, that such irrationality *is* possible, it is a challenge to see just where Socrates' ingenious refutations can be faulted.

To find Socrates apparently endorsing the view (the one he initially attributes to ordinary people, and uses against them) that pleasure is the sole good is itself surprising. Likewise the claim that the salvation of our lives is a kind of measuring knowledge – the ability to measure pleasures and pains correctly, and not to be taken in by illusions based on some pleasures being nearer than others. (Contrast Protagoras' more common-sense view, in his 'Great Speech', that the salvation of humankind lies in our sense of right and wrong.) Does Plato expect the reader to take seriously the idea that being good is just a matter of knowing what is and is not pleasurable? Critical opinion remains divided on the question of his (and Socrates') sincerity.

At all events, John Stuart Mill was right to see in this leading idea a precursor of his own views. In his *Utilitarianism*, he combines hedonism – the view that the only good is pleasure – with the claim that the right action is one which promotes the general happiness. Though this latter idea is not present in the *Protagoras* – which focuses on the agent's own pleasures, not on universal pleasure – Mill certainly found here the idea of a science of measuring and weighing up pleasures and pains. Hence his description (*Utilitarianism* (1861), chap. 1) of the *Protagoras* as presenting Socrates asserting 'the theory of utilitarianism against the popular morality of the so-called sophist'.

## The Meno

The *Meno* is often thought to mark a transitional point in Plato's writings. In part it resembles some earlier dialogues in which Socrates conducts an instructive but fruitless inquiry into some ethical concept, but it also introduces some themes which will be prominent in Plato's more mature philosophizing, such as the theory that learning is remembering, and the method of inquiring through a hypothesis. After an inconclusive and frustrating first third in which Socrates and Meno search for a definition of *being good*, new impetus to the inquiry is given with the startling suggestion that learning is really just *remembering* – the famous 'theory of recollection', which is thought to be Platonic, not Socratic, in origin, and which appears again in some later dialogues. The scene in which Socrates questions a slave on a geometrical problem is unforgettable, and raises – among other issues – the question of innate knowledge, something that has remained a hot topic of debate in all periods of philosophy. From that new impetus, the inquiry takes a more fruitful turn, though the earlier conclusions about being good, which seemed to be safe (that it is a kind of knowledge and can be taught) are overturned in the closing pages. Or are they?

Like the *Protagoras*, the *Meno* deals with the question – here posed right at the start by a young nobleman from Thessaly, Meno – 'How do people come to be good? By teaching, by their nature, or how exactly?' Socrates insists on first investigating *what being good is*, because, until they know that, there's no hope of knowing whether it can be taught. As in the *Protagoras*, the contested nature of being good is soon evident. Meno first links it to a person's role in life: being good, for a man, is a matter of ruling the city well, and of helping friends and harming enemies; for a woman, it is running the household well. Like many from a privileged background, Meno is keen to

believe that being rich and powerful is somehow linked with
being a good man, but he also readily accepts Socrates' prompts
to focus on ethical qualities, such as respect for what's right
and moderation (73a–b, 78d–e). The ultimately unsuccessful
examination of Meno on the question of what being good is,
which occupies the first third of the dialogue, has many features
in common with other, early dialogues such as the *Laches*
(what is bravery?) or the *Charmides* (what is moderation?).
The pattern is this: Socrates – who always insists on his own
ignorance – asks the question 'What is such-and-such?' The
other parties give answers which he criticizes, typically because
they list *many instances* of such-and-such and fail to give a
*single* account; because they leave out something essential (see
73a–b); and generally because they don't capture *the essence
of such-and-such* – what makes it what it is. After several failed
attempts by Meno to say what being good is, Socrates offers
sample definitions of shape and colour as a way of showing the
kind of account of being good he is after. These are of interest
in their own right, and the second definition of shape (as 'the
thing that borders a solid' [76a]) shows the clear influence of
the geometry that has come down to us under the name of the
later mathematician Euclid.

The search for definitions that give a thing's essence is
ascribed by Aristotle to the historical Socrates. It has remained
a key element in abstract philosophizing ever since, though it
has also come under fire, notably in the later philosophy of
Wittgenstein, who argued that we can understand concepts
perfectly well without a grasp of any single underlying essence
– something he thought was not there to be found. The task of
finding a single definition of being good – of being a good
person – is especially problematic, because it is what we might
call a 'thin' concept (that is, liable to being filled out in almost
any number of different ways, a feature that Meno illustrates
in his very first attempt to define it). Some recent moral philosophers have reversed Socrates' order of priority (see 79b–d)
and suggested that a better approach to this kind of task is to
explicate 'thin' ethical concepts, such as 'being good' or 'a right
action', in terms of what they call 'thick' concepts – concepts

with a fuller, more definite content – such as 'bravery', 'honesty', 'generosity' and so forth.

At any rate, in the *Meno*, all attempts to work out what being good is are found wanting, including perhaps the most promising one, offered by a poet (77b): 'to rejoice in what's fair and fine, and be able' – that is, to have honourable desires and goals in life, and to be able to achieve them.

Two of the ideas for which Plato is best known are the so-called 'theory of forms' and the notion that learning is really *remembering* – i.e. remembering things the soul knew before its incarnation in human form. These ideas are found together in his *Phaedo*, a work that refers back to the *Meno* and so must follow it. Our dialogue does not feature the 'theory of forms' – the thesis that true reality, and the objects of genuine knowledge, are things such as beauty itself and the good itself, which cannot be reached by the senses or by experience, but which must be discerned by purely intellectual means. Nonetheless, a focus on what has come to be called *a priori* knowledge (knowledge which does not depend on experience) is found in the most famous episode of the *Meno*, where Socrates questions one of Meno's slaves on a problem in geometry.

The episode is prompted by a puzzle known as Meno's paradox. Exasperated at their lack of progress, Meno raises difficulties for Socrates, who claims to know nothing at all about being good, yet still tries to find out what it is.

> But how can you try to find out about something, Socrates, if you 'haven't got the faintest idea' what it is? I mean, how can you put before your mind a thing *that you have no knowledge of*, in order to try to find out about it? And even supposing you did come across it, how would you know that *that* was *it*, if you didn't know what it was to begin with? (80e)

These are serious questions, and Meno scores a fair point against Socrates' constant affirmations of *total* ignorance. If Socrates really knows nothing at all about being good, how is it he even manages to discuss it, and to correct Meno every time he makes a suggestion about it? But Socrates treats Meno's question as if it were equivalent to a different, and much stronger, claim, that it is impossible for us to try to find out anything whatsoever (regardless of what we claim to know of it beforehand): we can't try to find out what we know (because obviously there's no point in finding out what we already know) *or* what we don't know (because then we don't know what we're trying to find out about). Socrates calls this a 'quibbler's argument', and indeed the second part is decidedly fishy.

But rather than dismiss this as a trick, Socrates uses the paradox about the impossibility of inquiry as a springboard from which to launch his theory of learning as remembering, at first via a myth, then through a bold demonstration. He tells Meno to choose a slave, to whom he sets the following rather difficult problem: How long is the side of a square that is double the area of a square whose sides are two feet long? The slave is shown why his first two answers (four feet long, three feet long) are wrong; Socrates finally helps him to the solution by drawing the diagonal (whose length is $\sqrt{8}$) of the original square and showing why that forms the side of a square double the area of the original one. On getting the slave's assent to this, he declares to Meno that these answers *were in the slave all along*; 'I, Socrates, didn't teach him anything.' And the reader is likely to protest: 'None of this shows the slave *remembering* the answer – rather, Socrates simply hands it to him on a plate. Why on earth should we think the slave knew or had true opinions about the answers *all along*? There's nothing special here, just Socrates explaining some geometry.'

This response is partly right, partly wrong. We're probably right not to accept the description *remembering*, much less agree that this establishes the further diagnosis Socrates gives, that the slave's soul was in possession of these truths before birth and indeed is immortal, ever-living. But, for all that, the episode shows that Plato is on to something important, a special kind of knowledge-acquisition. Even if the correct answer is in a sense provided by Socrates, the slave *can understand* why his first answers were wrong, and why the solution in terms of the diagonal is correct. He needn't take anything *on trust* from

Socrates. An uneducated but intelligent person could even work it out for himself, as Pascal is said to have worked out much of Euclidean geometry on his own in an attic when a small boy. What Plato is demonstrating – though Socrates describes it differently – are the human powers of reasoning, and the ability to extend one's knowledge from within oneself. Indeed, Plato himself inserts a very clear doubt about the more extravagant conclusions (86b), though in the later *Phaedo* the doctrine that the soul is ever-living is defended more fully with several arguments, together with a new version of the theory that learning is remembering.

The *Meno*'s 'demonstration' of pre-natal knowledge was tremendously influential on later philosophers who espoused the theory of innate knowledge, notably Leibniz, who admired Plato's 'beautiful experiment with the slave-boy' and thought its conclusions essentially correct, provided they were 'purged of the error of belief in the pre-existence of the soul'. Like Plato, Leibniz thought mathematical knowledge the best example of innate knowledge. What readers of Plato marvel at is the *Meno*'s assumption that truths about *being good* – what it is and how it is acquired – are also in some sense already in us when we are born, and as hard-and-fast as mathematical truths, and susceptible to the same kind of inquiry from 'within oneself'. Yet here too Plato may have an insight that is imaginative and in some ways correct, and one which modern thinking has taken up, but in rather different terms. Evolutionary psychologists hold that we are not ethical 'blank slates'; rather, our complex ethical intuitions are grounded in our evolved human nature, not acquired purely from experience.

The last stretch of the *Meno* presents a particularly sharp challenge to interpreters of Plato, since within a few pages we get an argument 'from a hypothesis' that being good is a kind of knowledge, and teachable, followed swiftly by a retraction, a new discussion and a new suggestion about being good. The ostensible conclusion of the work is that being good can't be taught since all the suggested candidates for its teachers – sophists, poets, decent people – turn out not to be successful teachers after all. Not being teachable, it can't be knowledge, so it must be more like correct opinion acquired by good fortune – a sort of divine fluke. On one line of interpretation, influenced by Plato's later work the *Republic*, which recognizes a sort of citizen-goodness possessed by non-philosophers, Plato here makes Socrates seriously propose this new way of being good, such that being good is not a matter of having knowledge but a set of true opinions which needs no profound intellectual inquiry. This picture of being good may have its merits, but there are clear indications in the text that Socrates is being tongue-in-cheek in proposing it (see 99c, 99d). Note that just after making the suggestion, he strongly insists that right opinion, while it has its uses, is less long-lasting and less valuable than knowledge, which requires a working out of why the thing known is true (98a).

A rival reading suggests itself. Perhaps Meno was too quick to accept Socrates' reversal of the earlier conclusion, the one arrived at by arguing 'from a hypothesis', that being good *is* knowledge and *can be* taught. Plato's readers who are familiar with some other works (*Protagoras, Euthydemus*) and who remember the earlier argument (77–8) that no one can want what they know will harm them, will recognize in the argument for the equation of being good with knowledge some familiar Socratic themes: being good always benefits you; only knowledge is consistently beneficial, since other good things (such as health, wealth and even quick-wittedness) can do you harm as well as good. When Socrates purported to think that an absence of conventional teachers proves a thing unteachable, perhaps he was testing Meno, testing him to see if he had retained the lesson from the experiment with the slave, that true teaching – certainly in the ethical sphere – is when you are helped to work out something for yourself, not when some paid teacher or other authority figure tries to din it into you.

# Further Reading

*Books marked with a dagger are accessible to the general reader
with no background knowledge of philosophy*

## Texts and Commentaries

Burnet, J., *Platonis Opera*, 5 vols (Oxford: Oxford University
Press, 1903). The Greek texts of *Protagoras* and *Meno* are
in vol. 3; a new edition is expected soon.

Adam, J., and A. M. Adam, *Platonis Protagoras*, 2nd edn
(Cambridge: Cambridge University Press, 1905). Text with
introduction and commentary (Greek-readers only); appendix on the Simonides song.

Bluck, R. S., *Plato's Meno* (Cambridge: Cambridge University
Press, 1964). Text with introduction and scholarly commentary (Greek-readers only); appendix on the geometrical
'hypothesis'.

Hamilton, E., and H. Cairns, eds, *The Collected Dialogues of
Plato* (Princeton: Princeton University Press, 1961). Includes
W. C. K. Guthrie's translations of the *Protagoras* and the
*Meno*.

Hubbard, B. A. F., and E. S. Karnofsky, *Plato's Protagoras:
A Socratic Commentary* (London: Duckworth, 1982). Translation with commentary in the form of questions.

Lamb, W. R. M., *Plato: Laches, Protagoras, Meno, Euthydemus* (London and Cambridge, MA: Harvard University
Press, 1924). Vol. 2 of the Loeb edn of Plato; a Greek text
and facing translation.

Sharples, R. W., *Plato: Meno* (Warminster: Aris and Phillips

Ltd, 1985). Greek text and facing translation, with introduction and commentary (partly) aimed at students of Greek.

Taylor, C. C. W., *Plato: Protagoras*, rev. edn (Oxford: Oxford University Press, 1991). Translation with useful philosophical commentary (Greek not required).

Thompson, E. S., *The Meno of Plato* (New York and London: Garland, 1980 [1901]. Text and commentary (Greek-readers only).

## Plato, Socrates and the Sophists (General)

Benson, H., ed., *Essays on the Philosophy of Socrates* (Oxford: Oxford University Press, 1992)

Diels, H., and W. Kranz, *Die Fragmente der Vorsokratiker*, 3 vols, 6th edn (Berlin: Zurich and Hildersheim, 1985). Contains the surviving fragments of the sophists (in Greek).

Dillon, J., and T. Gergel, *The Greek Sophists* (London: Penguin Classics, 2003).† Contains useful information on the sophists, Hippias, Prodicus and Protagoras.

Grube, G. M. A., *Plato's Thought*, with new introduction, bibliographic essay and bibliography by Donald J. Zeyl (Indianapolis: Hackett, 1980)†

Guthrie, W. K. C., *A History of Greek Philosophy*, vol. 3: *The Fifth Century Enlightenment* (Cambridge: Cambridge University Press, 1969). Also available in two parts: *The Sophists* and *Socrates*.†

——, *A History of Greek Philosophy*, vol. 4: *Plato: The Man and His Dialogues, Earlier Period* (Cambridge: Cambridge University Press, 1975)†

Irwin, T., *Classical Thought* (Oxford: Oxford University Press, 1989)†

——, *Plato's Ethics* (Oxford: Oxford University Press, 1989)

Kahn, C. H., *Plato and The Socratic Dialogue* (Cambridge: Cambridge University Press, 1996)

Kraut, R., ed., *The Cambridge Companion to Plato* (Cambridge: Cambridge University Press, 1992). Contains a large general bibliography.

Popper, K., *The Open Society and its Enemies, Vol. I: The*

*Spell of Plato*, new edn (London and New York: Routledge Classics, 2003)†

Robinson, R., *Plato's Earlier Dialectic*, 2nd edn (Oxford: Oxford University Press, 1953)

Taylor, C. C. W., *Socrates: A Very Short Introduction* (Oxford: Oxford University Press, 1998)†

Vlastos, G., *Socrates, Ironist and Moral Philosopher* (Cambridge: Cambridge University Press, 1991)

——, *Socratic Studies*, ed. M. Burnyeat (Cambridge: Cambridge University Press, 1994)

Waterfield, R., *The First Philosophers: The Presocratics and Sophists, Translated with Commentary*, Oxford World Classics (Oxford: Oxford University Press, 2000)†

Williams, B., *Plato: The Invention of Philosophy* (London: Phoenix, 1998). A short introduction.†

## Books and Articles Useful for Further Study of Protagoras

Davidson, D., 'How is Weakness of the Will Possible?', in *Actions and Events* (Oxford: Oxford University Press, 1980)

Gosling, J. C. B. and C. C. W. Taylor, *The Greeks on Pleasure* (Oxford: Oxford University Press, 1982)

Hutchinson, G. O., *Greek Lyric Poetry* (Oxford: Oxford University Press, 2001). Contains a text and commentary on the Simonides song.

Irwin, T., 'Socrates the Epicurean?', *Illinois Classical Studies* 11 (1986), pp. 85–112; also in Benson, 1992, pp. 198–219

Lombardo, S., and K. Bell, *Plato, Protagoras* (Indianapolis and Cambridge: Hackett, 1992). Translation with an introduction by M. Frede.†

Nussbaum, M. C., *The Fragility of Goodness* (Cambridge: Cambridge University Press, 1986)

Penner, T., 'The Unity of Virtue', *Philosophical Review* 82 (1973), pp. 35–68

Rudebusch, G., *Socrates, Pleasure and Value* (Oxford: Oxford University Press, 1999)

Vlastos, G., 'The Unity of the Virtues in the Protagoras', *Review*

*of Metaphysics* 25 (1971–2), pp. 415–58; also in *Platonic Studies*, 2nd edn, (Princeton: Princeton University Press)
———, ed., *Plato's Protagoras* (Indianapolis and New York: Liberal Arts Press Inc., 1956). Benjamin Jowett's translation, revised by M. Oswald, with an introduction by Vlastos.†

## Books and Articles Useful for Further Study of Meno

Bowra, C. M., *Pindar* (Oxford: Oxford University Press, 2000)

Burnyeat, M., 'Examples in Epistemology', *Philosophy* 52 (1977), pp. 381–98

Day, J. M., ed., *Plato's Meno in Focus* (London: Routledge, 1994). Translation and essays on several topics in the *Meno*.

Demas, P., 'True Belief in the *Meno*', *Oxford Studies in Ancient Philosophy* 14 (1996), pp. 1–32

Devereux, D., 'Nature and Teaching in Plato's Meno', *Phronesis* 23 (1978), pp. 118–26

Fine, G., 'Inquiry in the *Meno*', in *The Cambridge Companion to Plato* (Cambridge: Cambridge University Press, 1992), pp. 2002–26

Leibniz, G. W., 'Discourse on Metaphysics,' in *Philosophical Essays*, trans. R. Ariew and D. Garber (Indianapolis: Hackett, 1989)

Nehamas, A., 'Meno's Paradox and Socrates as a Teacher', *Oxford Studies in Ancient Philosophy* 3 (1985), pp. 1–30; also in Benson, 1992, pp. 298–316

Pinker, S. *How the Mind Works* (New York: W. W. Norton, 1997; London: Penguin Books, 1998)†

Scott, D., *Recollection and Experience: Plato's Theory of Learning and its Successors* (Cambridge: Cambridge University Press, 1995)

Vlastos, G., 'Anamnesis in the Meno', *Dialogue* 4 (1965), pp. 143–67; also in Day, 1994, pp. 88–111

Weiss, R., *Virtue in the Cave, Moral Inquiry in Plato's Meno* (Oxford: Oxford University Press, 2001)

White, N. P., *Plato on Knowledge and Reality* (Indianapolis: Hackett, 1976)

# A Note on the Translations

The text used for these translations is John Burnet's Oxford Classical Text (1903), except in a few places, which are marked with asterisks. There is a full list of these minor changes in the Appendix. The superscript numbers refer to endnotes, which contain historical and biographical information, as well as occasional philosophical points. The notes are mostly intended for students; I advise first-time readers to pay no attention to them. The dialogues are best read without interruption. The section breaks are my own, not Plato's, and the numbers and letters in the margins refer to pages and columns in the standard edition of Stephanus (Henri Etienne) of 1578. The alternative titles of the dialogues are ancient, but we do not know if they go back to Plato himself.

Roughly speaking, these translations are similar in both style and approach to the ones by W. C. K. Guthrie (1956) that they replace in this series, except that I have converted some of the traditional terminology into more modern equivalents. I mean traditional terms such as *virtue, vice, temperance, justice* (for *dikaiosúne*), *wisdom* (for *sophía*) and various others. So, in non-technical passages without much philosophical vocabulary, my translations are often fairly similar to Guthrie's; in the more philosophical passages they are very different, and in those places this version aims to be easier to understand. I have followed Guthrie in his (usual) aim of using clear, normal and more or less idiomatic English in the belief that that is the best route to accuracy.

The traditional renderings of Greek philosophical vocabulary just mentioned are not accurate or literal. No translator who uses them claims that they are. They are often based so closely on the original Latin translations that they require a knowledge of Latin to be fully understood. In other cases, they are the earliest English renderings, first devised in the sixteenth century. They are used, in spite of their inaccuracy, because of the important advantages of continuity with medieval philosophy, as well as with the huge body of scholarly commentaries and articles on these and other Greek texts. So I should alert the reader to the fact that I have decided not to use them here (or at any rate not all of them), and instead to translate the Greek terms into standard English, without any regard for either the Latin equivalents or the earlier English tradition. The same policy has been followed, to varying degrees, in other translations of Plato and seemed reasonable here partly because there are plenty of English translations of these two dialogues that do use the traditional terminology, so there wasn't any point in writing another one.

The problem with the traditional terms is that they are, in some cases, obsolete or moribund (or never truly adopted) as English words, and therefore very unclear (e.g. *temperance, virtue, munificence*), while in other cases they are widely used in modern English but have shifted in meaning over the centuries, to the point of being inaccurate in the special roles that we impose on them in these texts (e.g. *justice, happiness, wisdom, evil, fine, political*). The result of these two effects is a strange hybrid that tends to be extremely difficult to understand, making it correspondingly difficult to follow Plato's arguments at all closely.

Besides the Latin-based philosophical terminology, it is common in translations of Plato (even the most recent) to find a form of English that is, more generally, latinized. This is partly a matter of stylistic consistency, partly an aesthetic preference. By 'latinized' I mean, loosely, that high-register (often latinate) words and phrases – *tolerate, compose, proceed, engage in discussion, assert, investigate, inquire, respond, benefit, commit injustice* – are disproportionately favoured over more ordinary and common equivalents – *put up with, put together, go on, talk, say, look into, ask, answer, do good, do wrong*. In this version, I have also tried to present the tone and register of the original accurately, which means tending more to the second sort of vocabulary. Plato took care to capture the register and feel of spoken Greek, at least most of the time. Ideally, an English version should not contain too much that an English speaker could never say and should generally favour common forms. High-register English, by definition, contains things that we do not say, or which, if used in spoken language, make the speaker sound pompous or strange. That makes it a poor representation of Plato's style. A more demotic register also brings the small accidental bonus of often making the translation of particular terms more literal.

A few examples will show what I mean. Here the higher-register versions are taken from Guthrie's or Benjamin Jowett's translations of the two dialogues. The final column represents a style I try to use much, though not all, of the time.

| Greek | literal | Jowett or Guthrie | here |
|---|---|---|---|
| *légein* | to say | J, G: to assert, to contend | to say |
| *sképsasthai* | to look at | J: to investigate | to look into |
| *eis-bállein* | to throw in | G: to insert | to throw in |
| *apo-rrhoaí* | from-flowings | J, G: effluences | out-flowings |
| *dia-lek-tikó-teron* | more-talk-through-ish-ly | G: more conducive to discussion; J: more in the dialectician's way | in a more talk-it-through kind of way |
| *hos émoi dokeí* | As it looks to me | G: on my submission | if you ask me |

Plato's philosophy, in Greek, is (for the most part) clearly written and deliberately easy to follow, with strong and intelligible lines of thought, even if he sometimes makes very striking and unusual claims. For that reason, I take the goal of any translation of any particular term, phrase or idiom to be this: that it should systematically produce good sense from the sentences and arguments that use it in the original language. So it is the resulting English versions, taken in their entirety, that should make it clear why I opted for this or that particular word or idiom. All other arguments about how some term or other should be translated are secondary. To give one example: the common claim that *areté* means 'excellence' (rather than 'virtue') is sometimes regarded by students of Greek philosophy as being well established by a wide range of considerations, linguistic, historical and cultural. In reality, it is simply based on the fact that there are contexts in Greek philosophy and literature in which that translation seems to make good sense of the claims being made. But that means, obviously, that it is answerable to the same rule in the opposite case: in the many contexts in which it doesn't make sense of the claims being made, it should be regarded as a bad translation. The traditional vocabulary (for the reasons given above) often fails to make good sense; indeed it often fails to make any sense at all – but we make excuses for it, as we might for old friends, because of the powerful bonds of tradition and familiarity. So it is a misconception that using that vocabulary makes a translation more disciplined.

The principle adopted by some translators (for the sake of simplification, but also sometimes wrongly associated with literalism) that any important Greek term should always be translated the same way allows far too much freedom, in my view. In those common cases where a term has three or four distinct meanings or uses, that policy gives the translator licence to translate it in a single, reflex manner, regardless of how well that makes sense of the text.

Some translations, out of caution, leave actual Greek words in the English text or use established translator's jargon, or close copies of original idioms, that are unclear, because they simply stand in for the Greek rather than translating it. Those translations call on readers to have a pretty good knowledge of Greek vocabulary and idiom. My reservation about such translations is that they are therefore only fully intelligible to people who don't need them and probably aren't reading them; also, that it doesn't seem quite right for a translator to make so much effort to avoid translating. At the very least, that approach would be of no use to general readers. It was my aim to translate the text fully and to enable both the general reader and the student to follow the arguments closely and to understand these two very accessible dialogues without too much trouble. Accordingly, this version calls on readers only to know English and to rely fully on *my* understanding of Greek vocabulary and idiom. For that reason, and because of my modernization of the traditional vocabulary, some scholars might disagree with some of the renderings here. Disagreements of this kind between translators are inevitable, whatever the method of translation, and unremarkable. The Glossary, and several of the notes, try to alert scholarly readers to such things in more detail.

# PROTAGORAS

*or*
*The Sophists*

# Characters

SOCRATES, *a philosopher (here aged about thirty-five); the narrator of the main dialogue*

FRIEND, *to whom Socrates narrates the main dialogue*

HIPPOCRATES, *a young Athenian; a friend of Socrates; keen to be a pupil of Protagoras*

SLAVE, *doorkeeper of Callias*

*Inside Callias' house:*

PROTAGORAS, *a famous sophist from Abdera, just arrived in Athens (here aged about sixty)*

CALLIAS, *the richest man in Athens; stepson of Pericles; patron of sophists; Protagoras' host*

ALCIBIADES, *ward of Pericles; friend of Socrates (here aged about eighteen)*

CRITIAS, *a wealthy Athenian; an amateur philosopher; a friend of Socrates (also Plato's uncle)*

PRODICUS, *a sophist from Ceos; an expert on verbal distinctions; a friend of Socrates*

HIPPIAS, *a sophist from Elis; a polymath*

*Characters played by Socrates during the dialogue:*

SIMONIDES, *the famous songwriter from Ceos*

MOST PEOPLE, *'ordinary' people; only interested in pleasure (according to Socrates)*

A LOUT, *a rude interrogator, otherwise somewhat like Socrates*

ENDING, *the ending of the discussion, personified*

*The dialogue is set in Athens, in about 432 BC, just before the outbreak of the Peloponnesian War. Athens is at the height of its power in the Aegean and is the intellectual and artistic capital of Greece. The main dialogue takes place in a spacious, colonnaded courtyard inside Callias' house.*

FRIEND: There you are, Socrates.[1] Where've you been? Or is it   309 a
obvious? You've been hunting, haven't you? Chasing around
after that ripe young Alcibiades.[2] I don't blame you; I saw
him just the other day, and he's still a beautiful man, I'll give
you that – *man*, mind you, Socrates (just between you and
me): he's getting a little bit of a beard these days.

SOCRATES: So what if he is? I thought you were a fan of Homer
– and he says that 'a man with his first beard', like Alcibiades,   b
is at 'the high point of the charm of youth'.[3]

FRIEND: So what's new? Am I right? Have you just been with
him? How are things between you and the young man?

SOCRATES: Very well. At least, that was my impression; today
especially – he took my side and spoke up for me a lot . . .
yes, you're right: I have just been with him. But let me tell
you something really strange. He was there all right, but I
wasn't paying much attention to him, and pretty often I
forgot about him altogether.

FRIEND: No! How could something as serious as that have   c
happened between you two? You can't have met somebody
more beautiful. Not here in Athens, at any rate.

SOCRATES: I did – somebody far more beautiful.

FRIEND: I don't believe it! Was he a local or a foreigner?

SOCRATES: A foreigner.

FRIEND: Where from?

SOCRATES: Abdera.

FRIEND: And this foreigner struck you as so beautiful that he
seemed even more beautiful than Clinias' son?

SOCRATES: Well, of course he did. How could a supreme intel-
lect possibly fail to be something more beautiful?

FRIEND: Aha ... you've met some sort of intellectual, have
you?

d SOCRATES: Only the greatest intellectual alive today. That is,
if you think the greatest living intellectual is ... Protagoras.

FRIEND: You're kidding! Protagoras is here in Athens?

SOCRATES: Yes. He's been here for two days already.

FRIEND: And you mean to say you've been spending time with
him? Just now?

310 a SOCRATES: That's right. We had a long conversation.

FRIEND: Well why don't you sit yourself down and tell us all
about it! You can sit right here beside me; get the boy[4] here
to give you his seat – unless you're busy, that is.

SOCRATES: No, I'd be glad to. In fact I'd be grateful to you –
for listening.

FRIEND: Not as grateful as we'll be to you, for the telling.

SOCRATES: We'll be doubly grateful, then. All right, listen up.

Last night, a little bit before dawn, my friend Hippocrates –
Apollodorus' son; Phason's brother[5] – started making a huge
b racket banging on the door[6] with his stick; and when somebody
opened it for him, he came charging straight in and said, in a
loud voice, 'Socrates! Are you awake, or asleep?'

I recognized his voice and said, 'Hippocrates, is that you?
What is it? Has something happened?'

'No! – well, only something good!'

'That's a relief!' I said. 'So what is it? Why've you come
round so early?'

'Protagoras has arrived in Athens!' he said, standing beside
me.

'I know. He arrived two days ago,' I said. 'You've only just
found out?'

'That's right!' he said. 'I only found out yesterday evening.'

c      He felt around for the edge of my camp-bed[7] and sat beside
my feet.

'In the evening,' he said, 'when I got home, late, from Oinoë.
You see, what happened was, my boy, Satyros, ran away.[8] I

meant to tell you I was going to go after him, but something or other made me forget. And when I got home, and we'd had something to eat and were about to go to bed, that's when my brother tells me that Protagoras is here in Athens! And I was on the point of coming round to see you right away, but then I decided the night was too far gone; but as soon as I'd got some sleep and didn't feel so exhausted, I got up right away and came d over – so here I am!'

I could sense his enthusiasm and excitement. 'So what's this got to do with you?' I said. 'Protagoras isn't committing some kind of crime against you, is he?'

He laughed. 'Yes, he is, damn it! His crime is that he keeps his knowledge to himself and won't share any of it with me!'

'But of course he will. Just give him some money,⁹ and talk him into it, and he'll teach you everything he knows.'

'I wish – by all the gods! If only that were all it came down to! Believe me, I'd spend everything I have, and everything my e family has as well. But that's exactly why I've come round to see you: I want you to talk to him on my behalf. For a start, I'm too young. What's more, I've never even seen Protagoras or heard him speak. I was just a child when he was last in town. But everyone's talking about how great he is, Socrates, and how he's the most brilliant speaker! Come on, we should be on our way over there already – we've got to make sure we catch him before he goes out. I heard he's staying with Callias, 311 a Hipponicus' son.¹⁰ Come on, let's go!'

And I said, 'Hold on, Hippocrates. We can't go now – it's too early. Let's get up and go out here into the courtyard, and stroll around for a little while, until it gets light. Then we can go. In any case, Protagoras spends most of his time indoors, so don't worry; we're pretty likely to catch him before he goes out.'

Next, we got up and went out into the courtyard, and started walking around; and to get a clearer idea of Hippocrates' plan*, b I began sounding him out with a few questions.

'Tell me something, Hippocrates,' I said. 'Your idea is to go and see Protagoras, right now, and pay him a fee so he'll take you on – why? What is he? And what do you see yourself becoming, by being his pupil? I mean, look: suppose you'd been planning to go to your namesake, Hippocrates from Cos, the doctor, to pay him a fee for taking you on. If someone had said to you, "So tell me, why are you paying money to Hippocrates, Hippocrates? Because he's a . . . what?" What would you have said?'

c

'I'd have said, "Because he's a doctor."'

'"And what are you hoping to become?"'

'A doctor,' he said.

'And if you'd been planning to go to Polyclitus from Argos, or Phidias from Athens, to pay them your money, to take you on, and someone had asked, "What's the idea? Why give your money to Phidias and Polyclitus? Because they're . . . what?" How would you have answered?'

'I'd have said, "Because they're sculptors."'

'"And what are you hoping to become yourself?"'

'A sculptor, obviously.'

d       'Right; but in this case it's Protagoras you and I are going to see, and when we get there we're ready to pay good money for your tuition – our own money if it's enough to persuade him with, and, if it it's not, we'll spend our families' money too. So suppose someone saw how incredibly keen we were and said, "What's the idea, Socrates and Hippocrates? Why are you planning to pay Protagoras all this money? What is he?" Well,

e       what could we say? What do we hear people calling Protagoras, the way they call Phidias a sculptor and Homer a poet? Is there some other name like that for Protagoras?'

'A sophist, Socrates. People call the man a sophist.'

'Ah – a sophist. So that's why we're going to go and give him our money? Because he's a sophist?'

'Absolutely.'

'And what if someone asked you this as well: "And how

312 a   about you? What are you hoping to become, by going to Protagoras?"'

Hippocrates blushed[11] (there was just a little daylight by then – enough to give him away): 'Well, if those other cases are anything to go by, I'm obviously hoping to become a sophist!'

'You! A sophist? Wouldn't you be embarrassed, going around Greece presenting yourself as a sophist?'

'Well, of course I would! – I'd be lying if I said otherwise.'

'All right; so I take it you don't see the teaching you'll get from Protagoras as working the same way; you probably see it as being more like the things you were taught by your writing    b
teacher, or your guitar[12] teacher, or your athletics-trainer – because in each of those cases you didn't learn things with the idea of taking up their profession.[13] It was just for your education; the sort of thing you expect of any free citizen of independent means.'

'Yes, exactly,' he said. 'I think of the instruction that I'll get from Protagoras as being more like that sort of thing.'

'So do you realize what it is you're about to do? Or hasn't it occurred to you?'

'How do you mean?'

'Well, do you realize you're about to let a man take care of your soul?[14] A sophist, you say – but what *is* a sophist? I'd be    c
surprised if you knew. But if you don't know what a sophist is, then you also don't know whether you'll be handing over your soul to something good or something bad.'

'I think I know what a sophist is.'

'All right then; tell me what you think a sophist is.'

'I think,' he said, 'that a sophist, as the name implies, is someone who has *sophist*icated knowledge.'[15]

'All right; but isn't that something we can say about carpenters as well, or painters? – we could say they have "sophisticated knowledge" too. But if someone asked us, "In what area? What    d
is a painter's 'sophisticated knowledge' directed at?", we could say that it's directed at creating images; and we could say the same sort of thing for the rest of them. But what if someone asked, "So what about a sophist? What's his 'sophisticated knowledge' directed at?" What could we say? What does a sophist produce? What's he a master of?'

'I'm not sure what we'd say, Socrates – unless we'd say he's a master of making people skilled at speaking.'

'That may well be right,' I said, 'but it certainly isn't a full

answer, because it just raises the further question – what does a sophist make people skilled at speaking *about*?[16] Think of it this way: a guitarist presumably makes people skilled at speak-
e ing too – skilled at speaking about the same thing he teaches them – i.e., guitar-playing. Doesn't he?'

'Yes.'

'Right. So how about a sophist? What does he make people "skilled at speaking" about? Obviously it'd have to be whatever it is that he teaches them?'

'That would certainly make sense.'*

'So what is that? What's a sophist an expert at, and what does he make his pupils experts at?'

'Well, damn, you've got me there. I just don't know.'

313 a      So then I said, 'All right, how about this? Do you realize the kind of danger you'll be placing your soul in? I bet that if it was your *body* you had to hand over to someone, and you were taking a chance on its ending up in good or bad shape, you'd have thought really carefully about whether or not to go ahead with it; you'd have been asking your friends and family to give you their advice; you'd have spent several days looking into it. But here it's a question of something more precious to you than your body – your *soul*, the thing that determines (by turning out either good or bad) whether your *whole life* goes well or badly.[17] That's what's at stake here; and yet you didn't talk to your father about it, or your brother, or any of your friends, to
b see what they thought about whether or not it was a good idea to hand over your soul to this man who's only just arrived in town. You say yourself that you only heard last night that he was here, and yet here you are, at the crack of dawn, with no interest in talking about it, or asking my advice about whether or not this is something you should do, and you're ready to spend all your money, and all your family's money too, because you've already made up your mind that becoming Protagoras' pupil is something you've absolutely got to do. And this is a man you say you don't know, and haven't so much as spoken
c to, ever, and you call him a "sophist", but you obviously don't have any idea what on earth a sophist is – the thing you're planning to hand yourself over to.'

When he'd listened to all that, he said, 'Yes; from what you've been saying, that seems about right.'

'Well, would it be fair to say, Hippocrates, that a sophist is a sort of salesman or trader – trading in the goods that feed the soul? That's more or less what I think a sophist is.'

'But what is it that "feeds the soul", Socrates?'

'Well, the things we learn, of course,' I said. 'And we've got to be very careful not to let ourselves be duped by sophists when they're touting their wares – just like with people who sell food for the body: your ordinary merchant and market-trader. They're the same: they've got no idea, themselves, which of the d things they're selling are good or bad (for your body), but they'll claim it's all good, because they're selling it; and as a customer you don't know any better, unless you happen to be a trainer or a doctor. That's how it is with these people who deal in education, touring the cities like travelling salesmen, peddling their courses to anyone who wants them – sure, they'll talk up whatever it is they're selling; but it's pretty likely that some of them don't know which of the things they're selling are good or bad (for your soul). And the same goes for their e customers, unless you happen to be a kind of expert on the health of the soul.

'So, if you are in fact an expert on this sort of thing, and know which ones are good for you and which ones are harmful, there's no danger in your buying courses from Protagoras or from anyone else. But if you're not, then for heaven's sake be careful! Don't gamble – don't play dice with the most valuable 314 a things you've got! Remember, there are much higher stakes involved in shopping for education than there are in buying your groceries. The thing about buying food and drink from a street-vendor or a shop-keeper is that you can take it away in a separate container, which means that before you eat it or drink it, and take it into your body, you can go home, put it on the shelf and get someone who knows what they're talking about to help you decide what you should eat or drink, and what you shouldn't, and how much you should eat, and when you should eat it. So there's no great gamble just in buying it. But you can't take away learning in a separate container. Once b you've paid for it, you're forced to take it in with your very soul – to learn it – and go away either harmed by it or improved.

'So I think we should get some help looking into these things from people who've got more experience than us. We're still a bit young to be able to make such an important decision.

'But for the time being let's do as we planned and go and hear what the man has to say. And after we've spoken to him we can consult some of the other sophists as well. It isn't just Protagoras who's staying at Callias' place. Hippias from Elis is
c there, too, and Prodicus from Ceos, I think, and lots of other great intellectuals.'

So that's what we decided to do, and we started making our way over there.

And when we found ourselves in front of the door, we stood there and carried on a conversation that we happened to strike up on the way – we wanted to round it off before going inside rather than leave it unfinished, so we stood there, right in front of the door, talking things through until we'd come to an agreement. Now I think the doorman (a eunuch) had been eavesdropping on us; and chances are, with all the sophists who were staying there, he was pretty sick of people constantly
d coming to the house. At any rate, when we knocked on the door, he opened it, saw us and said, 'Oh no! Sophists! He's busy!'[18] And with that he very keenly slammed the door in our faces, with both hands, as hard as he could.

So we knocked again; and this time he kept the door firmly shut and answered like this: 'Didn't you people hear what I said? He's busy!'

'No, listen, my good man,' I said. 'We're not here to see Callias, and don't panic, we're *not* sophists. We're here because
e we want to see Protagoras. So go and let him know we're here.'

So eventually the man opened the door and let us in.

Once we'd got inside, we came upon Protagoras, walking up and down under the colonnade, with a number of people walking in a row on either side of him: on one side were Callias
315 a and his half-brother, Pericles' son Paralus, and Glaucon's son Charmides, and on the other side Pericles' other son Xanthippus, Philomelus' son Philippides, and Antimoerus

from Mendë – he's Protagoras' most famous pupil; he's training
with him professionally, with the idea of becoming a sophist
himself. And there were a number of others following along
behind them, listening to the talk, most of whom seemed to be
from out of town – the people Protagoras gathers from the
cities he passes through: he draws them with his spellbinding
voice, like Orpheus, and wherever the voice leads, they follow,    b
under his spell. But there were one or two Athenians in the
'chorus'[19] as well. And a particularly entertaining sight, I found,
was the way the chorus took great care to avoid getting in
Protagoras' way: each time he and the front row swivelled
around, the extra crowd of listeners split very neatly down the
middle, half to the left and half to the right, then swirled round
in an arc and took up their position at the back – it was
beautifully done.

'And whom next should I cast my eyes upon?'[20] (as Homer
says) if it wasn't Hippias from Elis. He was sitting in a high-    c
backed chair under the opposite colonnade; and sitting around
him on benches were Acumenus' son Eryximachus, Phaedrus
of Murrhinous and Androtion's son Andron, along with a
number of foreigners made up of Hippias' fellow Eleans and
various other people. They seemed to be quizzing Hippias on
natural science – stars and planets and so on – and he was
sitting there in his high-backed chair, passing out judgements,
explaining the answers to their questions.

'And then I caught sight of Tantalus as well!'[21] Yes, that's
right, Prodicus from Ceos was in town! He was there in a    d
building that Callias' father used to use as a storeroom, but
now, because of all the people that come to stay, Callias has had
it cleared out and converted it into rooms for guests. Prodicus
himself was still in bed, wrapped up in sheepskins and blankets
(a huge pile of them, as far as I could see); and sitting around
him on the beds next to him were Pausanias from Cerameis
and with Pausanias a teenage boy who, if you ask me, seemed
a fine lad, of good breeding; and he was certainly very easy on    e
the eye. I think I heard someone say his name was Agathon,
and I wouldn't be surprised if in fact he was Pausanias' sweetheart.[22] And besides the boy, I could see both the Adimantuses

(Cepis' son and Leucolophides' son) and various other people. But as for what they were talking about, from where I was standing outside I simply couldn't make it out, even though I was itching to hear what Prodicus was saying – he's a brilliant 316 a man, in my view, truly inspired – the problem was he's got such a deep voice that it set off a kind of rumbling echo inside the room, and I couldn't make out a word.

We'd only just come in when Alcibiades – beautiful Alcibiades, according to you, and I agree – arrived right behind us, along with Critias, Callaeschrus' son.[23]

Anyway, after we'd come in and spent a little time taking in the scene, we went up to Protagoras, and I said, 'Protagoras, I'd b like you to meet Hippocrates; he and I have come especially to see you.'

'And did you want to talk with me in private,' he said, 'or in front of the others as well?'

'We don't mind either way,' I said. 'Why don't we tell you why we've come, and then you can decide for yourself?'

'All right then,' he said. 'So why have you come?'

'Well, Hippocrates here is a local boy, Apollodorus' son – from a powerful and wealthy family; and in terms of his natural abilities, I'd say he's on a par with any of the young men his age. And his ambition, as far as I can tell, is to make a name c for himself in the city; and he thinks the best way to make that happen would be to spend some time as your pupil. That's it. So now you decide whether you think you should talk this over with us in private or in front of the others as well.'

'That's very thoughtful of you, Socrates – and quite right too. After all, if a man is an outsider, and comes into large and powerful cities, and persuades the very best of the young men in those cities to give up spending their time with anyone else, family or friends, young or old, and to spend their time with him alone, so as to better themselves under his influence . . . d well, a man who does that for a living has to watch his back. It can cause a lot of resentment, and hostility, and ill-will.[24]

'My own view is that the sophist's profession has been around for a very long time; it's just that people who practised it in the past devised covers for their profession and disguised it, because they were worried about offending people. Some of them used poetry as their cover: Homer, for example, and Hesiod, and Simonides.[25] Others used religious cults and oracular songs: Orpheus and Musaeus.[26] And I've noticed some people even use athletics-training, like Iccus from Taras, and another who's still alive and as good a sophist as any: Herodicus from Selumbria (although he's from Megara originally). And music; that was used as a cover by your own Agathocles – a great sophist – and by Pythoclides from Ceos,[27] and plenty of others. *e*

'All these people, I'm saying, hid behind the screens of these various professions, because they were scared of people's resentment. But in my case, that's exactly where I do things differently from all of them. And that's because I believe that *317 a* they completely failed to achieve what they intended: they never fooled the *powerful* people in their cities; and they're the only ones the disguises were aimed at (because, let's face it, ordinary people never notice anything anyway; they just repeat whatever's dictated to them by the powerful). Now if you try to get away with something, and don't succeed, and instead get found out, that shows it was a pretty dumb idea even to make the attempt, and it's bound to make everyone even more hostile, *b* because people look on someone who tries that sort of thing as being dishonest on top of everything else. That's why in my case I've followed the exact opposite path: I freely admit that I'm a sophist and that educating people is my job; and I believe that method of protecting myself – admitting what I do rather than denying it – is far better than theirs. And I've taken a number of other measures besides that, the result of which is that nothing terrible ever happens to me – touch wood – through my admitting that I'm a sophist. And I've been practis- *c* ing my profession now for many years.[28] I've been around for quite a few in total. I'm old enough to be the father of any one of you.

'So what I'd very much prefer, Socrates, if it's all right with you, is if we talked this over quite openly, in front of all the people here.'

So I said – because I had the suspicion that he wanted to

show off a bit in front of Hippias and Prodicus, make a big fuss
over the fact that a pair of his adoring fans had arrived – 'Why
d don't we invite Hippias and Prodicus over as well, and their
pupils, so they can all listen in.'

'By all means!' said Protagoras.

'In that case, would you like us to set up some chairs in a
circle,' said Callias, 'so you can hold the talk sitting down?'

That's what we decided we should do, and at the prospect of
listening to these great minds we all gladly took hold of the
chairs and benches ourselves,[29] and arranged them beside
Hippias (since that's where most of the benches already were);
and at the same time, Callias and Alcibiades brought Prodicus
e over, after getting him out of bed, along with Prodicus' pupils.

Once we were all sitting in a group, Protagoras began: 'Now
then Socrates, would you be so kind as to explain for the benefit
of those who've just joined us the question you raised a few
minutes ago when you spoke to me on the young man's behalf?'

318 a     So I said, 'I'll start from the same point as I did just a moment
ago, Protagoras – our reason for coming to see you. The situation is this: Hippocrates here is keen to become your pupil;
and he says he'd like to find out exactly how being your pupil
will affect him. What's he going to get out of it? That's really
all we wanted to say.'

Here's how Protagoras replied: 'Quite simply, my young
friend, if you become my pupil, what will happen is, the very
day you start your tuition, you'll go home better than you were
before; and the day after that the same thing will happen; and
with every single day that passes you'll constantly improve.'

b     When I'd heard that, I said, 'Well, no surprises there, Protagoras. I could have figured that much out. I mean, after all,
even you, in spite of your long experience and great knowledge,
even you would get "better" if somebody taught you something
you happened not to know anything about. That's not the
answer I'm looking for. Look, imagine Hippocrates here had a
sudden change of heart and wanted to become the apprentice
of that young painter who's settled in Athens just recently –
Zeuxippus from Heraclea – and suppose he went to him, the
c same way he's come to you, and heard the same thing he's just

heard from you, that with each passing day he'd "get better" and "improve", and followed that up by asking, "Yes, but better at what? What am I going to improve *at*?" Zeuxippus would be able to tell him he'd get better at painting. And suppose he signed up with Orthagoras from Thebes, and heard the same thing from him, and again asked what exactly he'd be getting better at, with each passing day, by being his pupil. He'd say, "better at playing the flute".[30] That's the kind of answer I want you to give my young friend, and me too, since I'm the one asking the question for him: "Hippocrates here, if   d he becomes Protagoras' pupil, will, the very first day he starts his tuition, return home better, and will improve like that with every passing day" – but better at what, Protagoras? Improve in what way?'

When Protagoras had heard what I had to say, he said, 'You put your question really well, Socrates. And I like giving answers to people who ask good questions. So – if Hippocrates comes to me, his experience will be quite unlike what would have happened to him had he enrolled with any of the other sophists. The fact is, other sophists abuse the young. They take young men who have specifically avoided skilled professions   e and thrust them, against their will, right back into mere skills – by teaching them mathematics, and astronomy, and geometry, and music' – and as he spoke he shot a glance at Hippias – 'but if he comes to me, he'll only be taught the thing he's come to me to learn. The course I teach is in good decision-making, whether it's in his personal life, where the question is how he can best manage his own household, or in public matters, where the aim is to make him as effective as he can be at handling and   319 a debating the affairs of his city.'

'Let me see if I follow what you're saying,' I said. 'It looks to me as if you're talking about civic and ethical know-how.[31] You're saying you actually undertake to turn people into good citizens.'

'That's exactly right, Socrates. That's precisely the service I offer.'

'Wow!' I said. 'In that case that's quite an impressive little skill you've got there – if what you're saying is true. Because

I'm going to be perfectly frank with you, Protagoras; the fact is, I always thought this was something people couldn't be
b  taught – of course, seeing as it's you saying otherwise, I don't see how I can possibly have any doubts. But I suppose I should explain my reasons for thinking this is something that can't be taught or . . . supplied from one person to another.

'The thing is, I look upon Athenians – as does everyone else in Greece – as being pretty smart people.[32] And I notice that when we come together for our public meetings, sometimes, if the city has to do something that involves, say, a building project, then it's the builders who are called in to give advice on the construction work; and if it involves making ships, then it's the shipbuilders – and it's the same with everything else;
c  everything, that is, that they think of as being teachable and learnable. And if anyone else tries to give them any advice, someone they don't recognize as a professional, then it doesn't matter how beautiful he is, or how wealthy, or how important his family is – they won't pay any more attention to what he has to say; they'll just laugh at him and heckle him, until the man trying to speak gets shouted down and backs off of his own accord, or the archers drag him away, or haul him out, on the orders of the presiding officers.

'So that's the way they do things when they're discussing something they think of as a matter of technical know-how. But when they've got to come to some general decision on how
d  our city should be run,[33] then anyone at all can get up and give an opinion – he could be a carpenter or a smith; a shoemaker, a shopkeeper or a shipowner; he could be rich or poor; an aristocrat or a nobody. And this time no one gets angry – the way they do in those other cases – no one complains that "he hasn't learned these things anywhere; he hasn't had a teacher; and now he's trying to tell us what to do!" – obviously because they don't think of this as something people can be taught.

'But don't think this only applies in the public domain. It's
e  the same with individuals: our best and smartest citizens are incapable of passing on to others what it is that makes them good.[34] Take Pericles, the father of these boys here: in areas

that called for teachers, he had the two of them very well educated; but as for his own kind of knowledge[35] – he isn't   320 a teaching them himself, and he hasn't handed them over to anyone to do it for him. Instead here they are, left to their own devices, roaming around like holy cows,[36] in the hope that they'll stumble their way into being good men, all on their own. Or how about what happened with Clinias, the younger brother of Alcibiades here? It involved Pericles again: he was Clinias' guardian[37] and became worried that Alcibiades might be a bad influence on him, so he snatched him away and set him down at Ariphron's, and started educating him there; but in less than six months he found the boy was just a hopeless case and sent him back to Alcibiades. And I could give you a number of other   b examples of people who, even though they're good people themselves, have never made any member of their own family a better man, or anyone else.

'So those are my reasons, Protagoras; reflecting on all of that, I take the view that you can't make someone good by teaching them.[38] Of course, now that I've heard you saying otherwise, I'm beginning to waver, and I find myself thinking there must be something in what you say, seeing as I look on you as someone of wide experience and great learning, and as an original thinker as well. So if you've got any way of making things a bit clearer for me and showing that being good is in fact something people can be taught, please don't keep it to   c yourself; show me why it's so.'

'Don't worry, Socrates,' he said. 'I'm not going to keep it to myself. But listen, would you all rather I explained things by plain argument, or shall I tell you a story, seeing as I'm the old man and you're the youngsters?'

A number of the people who were sitting around us said he should give his explanation whichever way he preferred.

'Well, in that case I think it would be more agreeable if I told you a story . . .'

'A long, long time ago,[39] there were only gods; there weren't yet any mortal kinds. And when the fated time arrived for them   d to come into being as well, the gods, working within the earth, began to mould them into shape from a blend of earth and fire (along with all the things that are a mix of fire and earth). And when they were on the point of bringing them into the light of day, they assigned to Thinxahead and Thinxtoolate[40] the task of embellishing the animals and handing out appropriate abilities to each. But Thinxtoolate asked his brother Thinxahead to let him do the handing out of things by himself. "Let me do it, and when it's done, come and check on what needs doing." He talked him into it and this is what he did:

e    'To some creatures he attributed strength without swiftness, the weaker ones he endowed with speed. To some he gave weaponry, while for the ones he'd given a weaponless physique, he devised some other ability for their survival: to those he'd wrapped in littleness, he gave the power to escape on wings or live below the ground; while for those he'd expanded to a great
321 a  bulk, he made that bulkiness the very thing that saved them. And he handed out everything else with the same sort of checks and balances, the aim of these devices being, so far, to ensure that no species should vanish from the earth. But once he'd provided the animals with sufficient means of avoiding a glut of mutual destruction, he also contrived ways of making their lives comfortable in the face of Zeus' seasons, by clothing them in thick coats of fur or toughened hides, which as well as being able to ward off winter's chill, and sufficient against the scorching summer heat, would also serve each and every creature, when it laid itself down to sleep, as its very own self-grown bedding. And when it came to footwear, some he
b    gave hooves, and some a covering of thick and bloodless skin. After that, he set about giving the animals various ways of feeding themselves. For some, it was the plants that sprang from the ground, for others the fruits or the roots of trees; and there were some that he allowed to devour other animals for their food, being careful, in those cases, to make the predators rare and with few offspring, but their prey abundant, so that their sheer numbers would be the means of their survival.

'Now Thinxtoolate wasn't all that smart, and before he knew

it he'd used up all the available abilities on the non-reasoning c animals. That meant he still had human beings on his hands, with no embellishments at all. And he simply didn't know what to do with them. And while he sat there with no idea what to do, along came Thinxahead to check the handing out of things, and he saw that while the other animals were all very carefully provided for, humankind was naked, shoeless, without bedding and defenceless. What's more, the day on which human beings had to come out of the earth and into the light was now at hand.

'Now it was Thinxahead who didn't know what to do: he couldn't come up with any way for human beings to survive, so he stole: he stole the technical ingenuity that belonged to d Hephaestus and Athena, along with fire (because there was no way anyone could possess it, or make any use of it, without fire) and he bestowed those gifts on humankind. By that means human beings at least acquired the kind of intelligence they needed to remain alive; but what they didn't have was civic and ethical intelligence. That was in the hands of Zeus, you see, and Thinxahead was no longer permitted to enter the citadel that was Zeus' residence – what's more, Zeus' palace guards were terrifying. But he was able to sneak into the house that was shared by Athena and Hephaestus, where the two of them spent their time happily plying their crafts, and he stole Hephaestus' e fire-based skills and various other arts that belonged to Athena, and gave them to humankind. And from that day forth the human race had what it needed to provide for itself and stay alive – though later Thinxahead was punished for his theft, so 322 a the story goes; all thanks to Thinxtoolate.

'So now that people had their little share of what is given to the gods, in the first place, on account of their connections in high places, they alone among living things had any notion of the divine, and they set about building altars and making statues of the gods. And as well as that, by using their ingenuity, they soon came up with words for things and formed articulate speech and invented shelters, clothes, shoes and bedding, and worked out how to grow their own food.

'Now, supplied with these advantages, in earliest times
b people lived scattered here and there.[41] There were no societies.
So they started being killed by the wild animals, since they
were weaker than them in every way, and their technical skills,
although up to the task of providing them with food, just
weren't good enough for the battle against the beasts (they
didn't yet have any civic and ethical know-how, remember; and
knowing how to fight a war is part of that). So they kept on
trying to find a way to gather into groups and defend themselves
by founding communities, but every time they came together,
they would do one another wrong, since they didn't have any
ethical know-how, and so they would scatter again and go back
to being slaughtered.

c 'At this point Zeus became worried that our species might
perish altogether from the earth, so he asked Hermes to take
down to people a sense of right and wrong.[42] This was to bring
order to societies, and to serve as the bonds for friendship and
love, and bring us together. So Hermes says to Zeus, "But how?
How am I supposed to give people this sense of right and
wrong? Should I hand it out in the same way we handed out
the technical skills? You remember how they were handed out.
One person with, say, knowledge of medicine is enough for a
large number of people who don't know anything about it; and
it's the same with the other skilled professions. So shall I put a
sense of right and wrong in human kind like that, or should
d I hand it out to all of them?" "Give it out to all of them,"
said Zeus.[43] "Every single one must have a share. The fact is,
there's no way societies could exist at all if only a few people
possessed a sense of right and wrong, the way it is with those
other skills. In fact, make it a rule, on my authority, that anyone
who proves incapable of acquiring some sense of right and
wrong must be thought of as a sickness to society and put to
death!"

'So there you go, Socrates, that's why it is that the Athenians
do things the way you say (along with everyone else): if they're
discussing how to be good *at carpentry*, say, or some other
technical field, then, yes, they take the view that only a few
people have the right to give them any advice, and if anyone

outside that small group tries to tell them what to do, they   e
don't put up with it (just like you say) – and that makes perfect
sense, if you ask me. But when it comes to discussing how to
be good *citizens*, which is entirely a matter of being ethical and   323 a
being sensible, it makes sense for them to accept advice from
any man at all, because they assume it's everyone's business to
be good in *that* way – or societies couldn't exist at all. There's
your explanation for that, Socrates.

'But I don't want you to think you're being duped; so let me
give you another reason for thinking that it is, definitely, a
universal assumption that everybody has some degree of respect
for what's right, along with the other parts of being a good
citizen.

'With all other forms of being good, as you pointed out
yourself, if you claim to be good at playing the flute, say, or
good at anything else technical when you're not good at it,
people will laugh at you or get angry; your family will take you   b
to one side and tell you to stop being crazy. But when it comes
to doing what's right and the other aspects of being a good
*citizen*, even if everybody knows you're a criminal, if you go
round telling the truth about yourself in public, then what
counts as sensible behaviour in the other cases – being honest
about yourself – in this case just looks like a kind of madness.
People feel that everyone has to claim they care about what's
right, regardless of whether they really do or not; if you don't
even make a *pretence* of being ethical\*, you must be crazy,
because it's a basic requirement, on absolutely everyone, that
they should have some degree of respect for what's right – or   c
they have no place in civilized society.

'So, what I've been claiming so far is that it's quite under-
standable that they take advice from anyone about how to be
a good citizen, because they believe that's something everyone
has their share of. What I'll try to show next is that they don't
believe it comes naturally, and they don't believe it develops all
by itself; they think that it's taught and that it comes about in
people, when it does, by care and effort.

'It's like this: there are defects that we think people have
because they're born that way or through bad luck. In those   d

cases, nobody gets angry or criticizes anybody; there's no
question of teaching people, or punishing them, to stop them
being the way they are; we just feel sorry for them. Nobody
thinks of treating ugly people in any of those ways, for example,
or people who are short or weak. What kind of thoughtless
idiot would do that? Everyone knows that it's just an accident
of birth whether we end up with those defects* or their opposites. But when it comes to things that we think are acquired
through effort, and practice, and teaching, this time, if someone
e     is found lacking and has the corresponding faults, we do
respond with anger, and criticism, and punishment. And among
those kinds of faults are disregard for what's right, and dis-
respect for religion, and, basically, everything that's the oppo-
324 a   site of being a good citizen. That's an area of life where everyone
gets angry with everyone, and everyone criticizes everyone else,
obviously because the attitude is that this is something you get
people to acquire by taking trouble over them and teaching
them.

'I mean, all you have to do is look at punishment, Socrates,
and ask yourself: What's the point of punishing people who do
wrong? That'll be enough on its own to show you that humane
societies, at least, believe that people can be "supplied with"
what it takes to make them good. The fact is, you don't punish
wrongdoers with the single-minded aim of paying them back
for the wrong they've done – not unless you're behaving like
b     an animal and taking some kind of pointless revenge. No, if
your aim in punishing someone is rational, then it's not about
the wrong that's been done – because after all, what's done is
done. It's for the future. The idea is to stop the person who did
wrong from doing wrong again, and to make other people think
twice when they see a wrongdoer punished. But that way of
thinking amounts to believing that you can make people good
through education – at any rate, you're punishing people as a
deterrent. So it follows that that must be the attitude of all
those who've ever punished anyone, whether in private or as
c     an institution. And, of course, as a rule, societies do punish
wrongdoers, and Athenian society is no exception. So by that
line of reasoning the Athenians must in fact be among those

who believe that people can be taught and "supplied with" what it is that makes them good.

'So now I've shown two things: first, that it's perfectly reasonable of your fellow citizens to listen to the opinions of a smith, or a shoemaker, on civic and ethical matters, and second, that they believe that being good is something people can be taught and "supplied with". I think I've demonstrated both those claims well enough.                                                                    d

'So let's see; that leaves you with just one more puzzle: you're puzzled about why on earth it is that, in all other areas, good people have their children taught everything that calls for teachers, and turn them into experts, but then *don't* make them any better than anyone else at being good the way they are themselves. All right; for this one I'm not going to tell a story; I'll just set out another argument.

'This is what you've got to think about: Is there, or is there not, one thing that every citizen has to have if society is to exist at all? That's the crucial question: the only one that's going to   e
clear away your puzzlement. – Yes, there is one thing that everyone's got to have, and it isn't skill as a carpenter, smith or potter. It's respect for what's right, and moderation, and   325 a
religiousness, and, in short, what I refer to as the quality of being a good man. That's what we've all got to have. That's the thing that every man has got to be exercising all the time, so that whatever he chooses to learn or do, doing it has to include being good (or else he shouldn't be doing it). And anyone who doesn't have it – man, woman or child – has to be taught and punished, until punishment turns them into a better person; and if they don't respond to being taught and punished, they have to be treated as incurable, and thrown out of society, or put to death. So if that's the way things are, if that's its nature,   b
and yet good people have their children taught everything else but *not* how to be good – think about how bizarre that makes good people. After all, we've just shown that they think of this as something that can be taught, in both the public and the private spheres. But if it can be taught and developed in a person, is it likely that they'd have their children taught all those other things (where there's no death penalty for not

knowing anything) and then not bother teaching them something where the penalty if they don't learn – if they don't
c  develop into good people – is death, or banishment; and as well
as death the confiscation of their property and basically, all in
all, the complete and utter ruin of their families? Do you think
they don't devote the utmost care and attention to it? Of course
they do, Socrates!

'In fact, right from when they're small children, and through
the whole of their lives, they teach them and set them straight.
From the first moment children can understand what people
are saying, their nurses, their mothers, their minders and even
d  their fathers – they all battle constantly to make sure the children turn out as good as possible, teaching them with every
single thing they do, with every single thing they say, showing
them: "That's right; that's wrong! That's well done! Shame on
you for that! The gods like this; the gods don't like that! Do this!
Don't do that!" And if the children do what they're told, fine;
but if not, then they treat them like timber that's crooked and
warped, and straighten them out – with threats and spankings.

'And then at the next stage, when they send them off to
school, they instruct the teachers to be far more concerned
with encouraging good behaviour in the children than with
e  teaching them to read and write or play guitar. So the teachers
take care of all of that, and once the boys learn the alphabet
and are just starting to understand written texts, just like when
they started to understand spoken language, the teachers set
out beside them, on their desks, the works of great poets for
326 a  them to read, which they force them to learn by heart; poems
that are packed with ethical guidance and full of stories which
praise and celebrate good men of the past, for the children to
look up to and imitate, to make them strive to be like that
themselves.

'And then there's the guitar teachers – it's the same story.
They take care to foster sensible behaviour and make sure the
boys don't do anything naughty. But as well as that, once the
children have learned to play the guitar, they teach them the
compositions of another set of great poets – songwriters –
b  setting their lyrics to music and forcing the boys' souls to

become familiar with rhythm and tuning, to make them more gentle, and with the idea that by having a better internal rhythm, and by being better tuned, they'll be useful to society in their speech and in their actions – because every area of life calls on us to have a good internal rhythm and to be in tune within ourselves.

'And then, of course, on top of all that, the parents even send them off to trainers, so that they'll have healthier bodies to be the servants of their healthy souls, and so they won't be forced by poor physical condition into losing their nerve, not just on    c the battlefield but in their other actions too.

'Now the people who do these things more than anyone else are just the people who *can* do them more than anyone else – and the people who can do them the most are simply the people with the most money. So it's their sons who start going off to school at the earliest age and who are the last to finish with teachers. But even when they do finish with teachers, society takes over; society makes them learn its laws and live their lives according to the standards set by those laws, so that they aren't left to work things out for themselves and act just any old how.    d It's exactly like the way that teachers who are teaching boys to write will trace out lines with the stylus (nice and light) for the ones who've not yet got the knack, then hand the writing tablet back and make them write by following the guides; society's the same: it draws up its "guidelines" – its laws, devised for us by good people in the past – and it forces people both to govern, and to accept government, according to those laws; and anyone who strays outside the law, it punishes. And the name used for that kind of punishment here in Athens, and in lots of other places, is "straightenings",[44] because the idea is that the penalty    e straightens you out.

'So, Socrates; with all this trouble being taken, both privately and publicly, to make people good, do you really find it so surprising, are you really so baffled about whether being good is something that can be taught? The fact is, it would be far more surprising if it *weren't* something that could be taught.

'So in that case why is it that fathers who are good men so

often have sons who turn out not to be much good? Let me explain that one. There's really nothing in the least bit surprising about this if what I was saying earlier on is right – that when it comes to this particular field, the field of being good

327 a people, everyone has to be an expert[45] if society is going to exist at all. Look, assuming that what I'm saying is right – and it definitely is right – just do this thought experiment. Put some other form of behaviour in its place, or something else that people learn: imagine, say, that it was impossible for society to exist at all unless we were all flute players, every one of us as good a flute player as they could possibly be; imagine that everyone, in public and in private, was always teaching everyone else how to play the flute and getting angry with anyone who didn't play it well; imagine that this was something everybody freely gave advice on, just as in the real world everybody freely gives out their opinions about what's right and what's

b lawful (no one keeps what they know a secret, the way they do in the skilled professions – presumably that's because we benefit from each other's respect for what's right, and from people being good *to one another*; that's why everyone's so keen to tell everyone else, and teach everyone else, what's right and what's lawful). Imagine that was the situation with flute-playing; suppose we were all highly motivated to teach one another, and entirely free with our advice; do you think the sons of good players would be any more likely to become good players than the sons of bad players, Socrates? No, I don't think so. What you'd actually find is that where a man happened to have a son with a natural talent for playing the flute, that boy

c would grow up to be a famous player; whereas if a man's son lacked the natural talent, he'd grow up an ordinary player. And plenty of times the son of a good player would turn out to be nothing special, and plenty of times the opposite would happen. But of course, they'd all at least be flute-players; they'd all be reasonably good, compared with non-players, compared with people with no knowledge of playing the flute at all. That's how it is in the real world too; what you've got to realize is that the person who strikes you as the most completely unethical out of those who've been brought up in a law-abiding, humane

society is actually ethical – an expert in that field – if he's to be
judged alongside people with no education, no judicial system,                d
no laws, no constraint of any kind constantly forcing them to
care about being good – some gang of savages, like the ones
Pherecrates[46] had in the play he put on at the Lenaea festival
last year. You can be quite sure that if you found yourself
surrounded by people like that, people like those monsters in
that chorus, you'd be more than happy to run into a Eurybatus
or a Phrynondas;[47] you'd find yourself longing for the kind of
immorality you find in people here! Crying out for it!

  'But as it is, Socrates, you're spoiled – spoiled by the fact that    e
everybody teaches us how to be good, every single person
teaches it as much as they possibly can; and you can't see
anyone doing it. It's just the same as if you tried to find out
who teaches us to speak Greek. You wouldn't find a single          328 a
teacher. Or if you tried to find out who could teach our craftsmen's sons – teach them that same craft they've learned from
their fathers, as far as their fathers could teach it, and their
fathers' friends who practise the same craft. If you said, "But
who could we find to teach them besides them?" I think it
would be hard to come up with anyone – for those boys; but it
would be perfectly easy to find teachers for people who don't
practise the craft. That's just how it is with being good, and
other things as well. The fact is, if you can find a man who's
even just a little bit better at advancing someone towards being
good, that's really the most we can ask for. And that's exactly       b
what I think of myself as being – one of those people: I believe
that when it comes to helping someone become a good and
decent man, I can offer something out of the ordinary and
worth the fee that I charge, or even more – so that people
who've been taught by me will feel it's been a bargain. That's
why I've set up my own special method of charging my fee,
which works like this: when someone's taught by me, if they
want to, they pay the sum of money that I charge; but if they
don't want to do that, they can go to a temple, state under oath      c
how much they think the teaching was worth and leave an
offering of that amount.

  'So there you are, Socrates. That's it. I've told my story, and

I've set out my argument – I've shown that being good is
something people can be taught, and that the Athenians believe
it's something that can be taught, and that there's nothing at
all surprising about the fact that the sons of good people can
turn out bad, and the sons of bad people can turn out good –
after all, even Polyclitus' sons, who are the same age as Paralus
and Xanthippus here, aren't a patch on their father,[48] and the
same goes for various sons of artists and craftsmen – although

d   it really isn't fair to lay the same charge against these boys here.
In their case we still have great expectations;[49] they're only
young, after all.'

Protagoras, after this long and wonderful performance, broke
off from his speech. And for quite some time I just sat there
gazing at him, mesmerised, waiting for him to say something,
longing to hear more! But once I realized that he really had
entirely finished, it was as though I had to struggle to regain
my senses, and I turned to Hippocrates, and said: 'Son of
Apollodorus, I can't begin to tell you how grateful I am to you
for talking me into coming along with you – I really appreciate

e   having heard the things I've just heard from Protagoras. Because
up until now I didn't think it was through other people's care
and attention that good people become good people. But now
I'm convinced ... except, that is, for one little thing that's
bothering me – but I'm sure Protagoras will easily clear it up
with some extra information, seeing as he's explained all these
other things so thoroughly. I mean, no doubt if you consulted

329 a  any one of our leading orators on these same questions, you'd
hear a similar sort of speech; from Pericles, say, or from any of
those men who are good at making speeches. But here's the
thing: if you go and ask one of them some follow-up question,
well, you might as well be talking to a book. They're incapable
of answering you or of asking anything themselves. If you ask
even some minor question following up on something they've
said, they're like bronze bowls, which *bong* when you tap
them, and go on and on bonging until you grab hold of them:

b   tap a politician with some little question, and he drones on
and on, endlessly. But Protagoras here – yes, he can produce

long, stylish speeches, as what we've just heard shows; but
he's also capable of giving precise answers when he's asked
particular questions, and of asking questions himself and having the patience to consider the replies – a rare package of
talents!

'So, Protagoras; in this case there's just one little thing leaving
me short of being completely satisfied – if you could just answer
the following question. You say being good is something people
can be taught, and if there's anyone I'm going to believe about
that, it's you. But there was something in your talk that rather
puzzled me, and I'd just like you to fill in the little gap it left in   c
my thoughts. You said that Zeus sent humankind a sense of
what's right and a sense of wrong, and then again at various
points in your arguments you talked about "respect for what's
right" and "being sensible" and "religiousness", and implied
that all these things together made up a single thing – being
good. Well, that's what I want you to go over for me in more
detail. Explain: is the idea that being good is a single quality,
and that respect for what's right, being sensible and religiousness are parts of it, or are these things that I've just mentioned all just different labels for one and the same thing? That's   d
what I'm still missing.'

'Oh, well, anyone could answer that one easily, Socrates:
being good is a single quality, and the things you're asking
about are parts of it.'

'Do you mean in the way parts of the face are parts – the
mouth, and the nose, and the eyes, and the ears – or more like
parts of gold, where the parts don't differ in any way either
from one another or from the whole chunk, except by being
bigger or smaller parts?'

'I'd say in the first way, Socrates; same as the relation between
the parts of the face and the whole face.'                              e

'So does that mean,' I said, 'that people can get these parts
of being a good person separately, with some people having
one part and some people having another, or is the idea that if
you've got one part, you're bound to have all of them?'

'No, not at all,' he said. 'After all, there are plenty of people
who are brave but don't care about what's right, and then

again plenty of people who care about what's right but lack knowledge.'

330 a    'Oh – so are those parts of being good as well, having knowledge,[50] and being brave?'

'Absolutely. In fact having knowledge is the most important part of all.'

'And each one of them is something quite distinct from the others?'

'Yes.'

'Does each of them also have its own particular role? I mean, like the way it is with the parts of the face: the eyes aren't *like* the ears, and their *role* isn't the same either; in fact none of the parts of the face resembles any other, either in terms of its role or in other respects. Is that how it is with the different parts of being good, too? Does no part of it resemble any other part,
b    either considered in itself or in terms of its role? Or is it obvious that that's the way it is – if our "parts of the face" analogy is a good one?'

'Yes, that's how it is, Socrates.'

And I said, 'So that means no other part of being good is like knowledge, and no other part is like respect for what's right, and no other part is like bravery, and no other part is like being sensible, and no other part is like being religious?'

'Yes, that's right.'

'All right then,' I said. 'Let's both of us think a bit about what each of the parts is like. First I want us to think about
c    this: respect for what's right, is that a thing, or is there no such thing? I think it's a thing.[51] How about you?'

'I think so, too,' he said.

'Right. So what if someone said to you and me, "All right, Protagoras and Socrates, in that case tell me this; this thing you've just called "respect for what's right", is it itself something right or wrong?" My answer would be that it's right. What would your vote be? The same as mine, or not?'

'Same as yours,' he said.

'So respect for what's right is, typically, something that's right; that's what I'd say in response to the man asking the
d    question. You'd say the same?'

'Yes.'

'Right. Now suppose after that he asked, "And you also talk about religiousness?" Presumably we'd say we did?'

'Yes.'

' "And do you claim that that's a thing as well?" We'd say we did. Right?'

He agreed.

' "And this thing, itself, do you think of it as being, typically, something that's against religion or something that's required by religion?" I'd be pretty annoyed by that question. I'd say, "What a shocking thing to ask, man! It'd be pretty hard to find anything else that was required by religion, if even *religiousness itself* turned out not to be required by religion!" How about   e
you? Wouldn't you answer like that?'

'Absolutely.'

'All right, now suppose after that he kept on at us and said, "So what was it you were saying just a moment ago? Maybe I didn't hear you properly. I thought you said that the relationship between the various parts of being good were such that no part was like any other." I'd say, "Well, you heard everything else right, but if you think it was me who said that, you heard wrong. That's something Protagoras here said in his replies; I   331 a
was just asking the questions." So then suppose he said, "Is what this man here says true, Protagoras? Is it you who say that no part of being good is like any other part? Is that your claim?" How would you answer?'

'Well, I'd have to admit it, Socrates,' he said.

'In that case, Protagoras, how are we going to answer the man, now that we've agreed on all of that, if he follows up with this: "So that means you're saying that being religious is not, typically, right; and doing what's right[52] is not, typically, something required by religion; in fact it's typically *not* required by religion; and being religious is, typically, *not right* – so in fact it's *wrong*, and doing what's right is *against religion*! Is that what you're saying?"[53] How are we going to respond? I   b
mean, speaking for myself, I'd say that doing what's right is required by religion, and that being religious is something right. And if I had to speak for you I'd give exactly the same answer,

if you let me – i.e. that either righteousness and religiousness are the same thing, or they're about as similar as any two
things can be, and that it's certainly the case that respect for
what's right is something like religiousness, and religiousness is
something like respect for what's right. So you'd better decide
if you want to veto that reply, or if you think the same way as
me.'

'I'm not at all convinced the question's so straightforward,
c Socrates, that I can just agree that respect for what's right is
something religious and religiousness something right. I think
there's a difference between them.* But what does it matter? If
you like, let's say respect for what's right is required by religion,
and that being religious is something right.'

'No, hold on,' I said. 'I've got no interest in investigating in
this "if you like" and "if that's what you want" kind of way;
it's the real you and me I want to test. And what I mean by
"the real you and me" is that I think the best way of testing out
d your claim would be if we left this "if you like" business out of
it entirely.'

'Well, all right,' he said, 'yes, there's some similarity between
respect for what's right and religiousness. I mean, for that
matter, just about anything is similar to anything in some
respect or other. I mean, there's even a sense in which black is
like white, and a sense in which soft is like hard – some respect
in which all the things we take to be total opposites of one
another are alike. Even the parts of the face, which a moment
ago we stated had different roles, and which we said were all
unlike one another – there are certainly some respects in which
they resemble one another, a sense in which each one is like the
e others. So on that basis you could argue, if you wanted to, that
they're all "like" one another as well. But you really shouldn't
call things "alike" just because they've got some point of similarity (or "different" just because they differ in some respect),
even when the point of similarity is a minor one.'

I was pretty surprised by that, and said, 'Is that really how
you see the relation between what's right and what's required
by religion? You think there's only a minor point of similarity
between the two?'[54]

'No. No, not at all,' he said. 'But then I don't think what you    332 a
seem to believe, either.'

'Well, look,' I said, 'since you seem a bit uneasy with that
particular question, we can just drop it. Here's something else
you talked about that I'd like us to look into. Do you think
there's such a thing as being stupid?'
    'Yes.'
    'And isn't having knowledge its exact opposite?'
    'Yes, I'd say so.'
    'And would you say that when people do things the right
way, so that what they're doing benefits them, they're acting
sensibly in acting that way? Or the opposite of sensibly?'
    'Sensibly.'
    'And they're acting sensibly because of their good sense, right?'   b
    'Obviously.'
    'And people who do things the wrong way are thereby acting
stupidly, and not being sensible?'
    'Yes, I agree,' he said.
    'So in other words, acting stupidly is the opposite of acting
sensibly?'
    'Yes.'
    'Right; and when people do things stupidly, they do so out
of stupidity, and when they do things sensibly, they do so
because of their good sense, yes?'
    He agreed.
    'All right; and if you do something with strength, you're
acting strongly; and if you do something out of weakness,
you're acting weakly. Yes?'
    'Yes.'
    'And if you do something with speed, you're doing it fast;
and if you do something with slowness, you're doing it slowly,
right?'
    'Yes.'
    'And in general, actions performed in the same way are    c
actions caused by the same quality; and actions performed in
opposite ways are actions caused by opposite qualities, right?'
    'That's right.'

'Now how about this,' I said. 'Do we call some things beautiful?'

'Of course.'

'And is there any opposite of what's beautiful besides what's ugly?'

'No.'

'What about good? Are some things good?'

'Yes.'

'And does what's good have any opposite besides what's bad?'

'No, it doesn't.'

'And is there such a thing, in sound, as high pitch?'

'Of course.'

'And that doesn't have any opposite besides low pitch, does it?'

'No.'

'So it looks like each thing that has an opposite has only one opposite and no more than one. Right?'

He agreed.

d     'All right then,' I said, 'let's just run back over what we've agreed so far. We've agreed that any one thing has no more than one opposite.'

'Yes.'

'And that two actions performed in opposite ways are actions caused by opposite qualities. Right?'

'Yes.'

'And we've also agreed that if you do something stupidly, you're acting in the opposite way to acting sensibly.'

'That's right.'

'And that if you do something sensibly, your action is a result of good sense, while if you do something stupidly, your action is caused by stupidity.'

He went along with that.

e     'So if you're acting in the opposite way, your action would have to be being caused by an opposite quality. Right?'

'Yes.'

'And one action is caused by stupidity, the other by good sense?'

'Yes'

'Opposite kinds of action?'

'Absolutely.'

'So, caused by opposite qualities?'

'Yes.'

'So stupidity is the opposite of good sense?'

'Looks like it.'

'Now, do you remember we agreed before that being stupid was the opposite of having knowledge?'

He admitted it.

'And that each thing had only one opposite?'

'Yes, I remember.'

'So which claim are we going to give up, Protagoras? The 333 a claim that each thing has only one opposite or the earlier claim, according to which having knowledge and being sensible are two distinct things, and each is a separate part of being good, and that as well as being two distinct things they're not even like one another, either in themselves or in terms of their role – like the parts of the face? What do you think? Which claim do we let go? After all, we certainly can't make both claims together very harmoniously; they're not really singing in unison, or "in tune" with one another, are they? How could they be, if we're sure that any given thing can have only one opposite and no more, and yet stupidity, which is one thing, seems to b have two opposites – knowledge *and* good sense? Is that right, Protagoras? Or have I missed something?'

He agreed – very grudgingly.

'So doesn't it look as if being sensible and having knowledge may just be one and the same thing? And earlier on it looked as if doing what's right and being religious were practically the same thing as well.'

'Come on, Protagoras,' I said, 'let's not give up! Let's carry on and look into the rest of these things as well. Tell me, do you think if you do wrong to someone, you can be acting sensibly in the very fact that you're doing them wrong?'                          c

'Personally, Socrates, I'd be ashamed to agree that that was the case, although certainly there are lots of people who think so.'[55]

'All right, so shall I direct the discussion at those people or at you?'

'If you like,' he said, 'start off by making that claim the target of your discussion – the claim made by most people.'

'It doesn't make any difference; as long as you answer the questions, I don't mind whether you actually believe what you're saying or not. It's the idea itself I want to examine – mind you, you and I, questioner and answerer, may also find ourselves being examined in the process.'

d        Now, at first, Protagoras started making a fuss – he complained that the idea was one he 'felt uneasy with' – but eventually he agreed to answer the questions.

'All right,' I said, 'let's start again. Do you think that sometimes people are being sensible in doing wrong?'

'Let's say so,' he said.

'And by "being sensible" you mean exercising good sense?'

'Yes.'

'And by "exercising good sense" do you mean that in doing something that's wrong, they're making a smart decision?'

'Let's say so.'

'And is that if they do well out of their wrongdoing, or if they do badly out of it?'

'Only if they do well out of it.'

'All right. Now, you think of some things as being good for us?'

'Yes.'

'And could we say,' I said, 'that good things are things that are beneficial to people?'[56]

e        'Well, yes, but there's more to it than that!' he said. 'I might call things good even if they aren't of any benefit to people whatsoever.'

I got the sense that Protagoras, by this point, was a bit prickly, and riled-up, and taking the questions in a ready-for-battle kind of way. So when I saw that was the mood he was in, I thought I'd better be careful and ask my next question very gently. 'How do you mean, Protagoras?' I said. 'Do you mean, things that

334 a   aren't of any benefit to any human being, or even things that

aren't beneficial *in any sense at all*? Do you call things like that "good" as well?'

'Well, of course not! Look, what I'm saying is, I can think of plenty of things that aren't beneficial to human beings – certain kinds of food, drinks, drugs, countless other things – and other things that are; and then some things aren't harmful or beneficial *to human beings* but are beneficial to horses; or only to cows; or to dogs. Then again, there are things that benefit none of those but do benefit trees. And some things are good for the roots of the tree but bad for the leaves. Take dung. Dung is good for any plant if you lay it over the roots, but if you go and pile it over the buds and young shoots, it invariably destroys them. Or olive oil: it's the worst thing possible for all species of plants and extremely damaging to the hair of all animals apart from human hair, but its effect on human hair is healthy, as well as on the rest of the body. Yet even then – so complex, so variable a thing is what's "good" – it's only good for the outside of the human body; the very same thing is extremely bad for the inside of the body; and that's why all doctors tell their patients not to put olive oil in the things they're going to eat, except in the smallest possible amounts – just enough to extinguish the unpleasant effects that foods and sauces can have on the senses of the nose.'

When he'd said all that, the people who were there burst into rowdy applause; they thought it was a great speech. And I said, 'Protagoras, the fact is, I'm a bit forgetful, and if someone makes long speeches at me I tend to lose track of what it is we're talking about. Now look; imagine I happened to be a bit hard of hearing. If you were going to carry on a conversation with me, you'd understand that you had to speak a bit louder than you do to everyone else. It's the same here: you've met someone who's a bit forgetful, so you've got to trim your answers for me, and make them shorter, if you expect me to keep up.'

'So what exactly do you mean when you say I have to make my answers "short"? Am I supposed to make them shorter than they need to be?'

'No, of course not,' I said.

'So they should be as long as they need to be?'

e    'Yes.'

'So does that mean as long as *I* think they need to be, or as long as *you* think they need to be?'

'Well, what I've heard people say,' I said, 'is that you have the ability – which you can also teach to other people – to take a given subject and talk about it either at great length, if that's what you feel like doing, such that you simply never run out of 335 a things to say, or in brief, so that nobody could make the same point more neatly. So all I'm saying is, if you're going to carry on a discussion with me, I'd like you to use the second method, please – keeping it short.'

'Look, Socrates,' he said, 'I've entered into contests of speech and argument with a lot of people before now, and if I'd always done what you're telling me to do – conducted the discussion on my opponent's terms – I'd never have been thought any better than the next man, and "Protagoras" would never have become a household name throughout Greece.'

At that point . . . because I sensed that he hadn't been very b happy with the way he'd handled his answers so far, and that if he had any choice in the matter he'd refuse to carry on the talk as the person answering the questions . . . I decided there was no point in my participating any further in the meeting.

'You know what, Protagoras,' I said. 'I have no wish for the meeting to carry on in a way that's not to your liking, either. Let me know when you feel like talking with me in a way I can follow. I'll talk with you then. Remember, you can hold conversations in either style – long speeches or keeping it short; that's what people say, and you say the same yourself. That's c because you're a smart guy. As for me, I just can't cope with these long speeches. I wish I could! But the fact is, you're the one who can do things either way, so it's you who needed to make the concessions, if we were going to carry on with our talk. But never mind; seeing as you don't want to, and since I've got something else I have to do and wouldn't be able to hang around while you reeled out long speeches, I'll be off. The fact is, there's somewhere I really must be going[57] – I mean,

don't get me wrong: I'd probably have quite enjoyed listening
to your long speeches as well.'

As I finished speaking, I started getting up to leave; and as I
was getting up, Callias grabbed hold of my arm with his right
hand and with his left hand took hold of my cloak – like that       d
– and said: 'No, Socrates! We're not going to let you go! Our
talks simply won't be the same without you! I'm asking you to
stay, for our sake. As far as I'm concerned, there's nothing I
would enjoy listening to more than you and Protagoras talking
something through. Please, Socrates; do us all a big favour.'

And I said – and by this point I'd already got up to leave –
'Callias, I've always been impressed by your enthusiasm for
philosophy, and I really do appreciate it now, as well – thank
you. So I'd be only too happy to oblige . . . if what you were       e
asking for were possible. But the fact is, you might as well be
asking me to run as fast as Crison, the runner from Himera, at
the peak of his form, or to run a whole race keeping pace with
some long-distance runner or all-day courier – if you wanted
me to do that, I'd say, "Look, nobody would like me to run as       336 a
fast as those guys more than I would! But the plain fact is, I
can't. So if you want to watch Crison and me running side by
side, you'll have to ask him to ease down to my speed. Because
I can't run fast, but he *can* run slowly." It's the same here; if
you're so keen on listening to me and Protagoras, you'd better
ask him to carry on answering my questions the same way as
he did at first – with short answers that stick to the question.
Otherwise, I can't see how our discussion can possibly work. I       b
mean, I always thought that actually engaging with one another
and talking things through was something different from
making long speeches.'

'But don't you see, Socrates?' he said. 'I think it's fair enough
of Protagoras to say he should be allowed to talk with you in
whatever way he likes, and you in whatever way you prefer.'

Here Alcibiades broke in: 'No, Callias. That's not right.
Look; Socrates here admits that long speeches aren't his thing,
and in that department he's happy to give up the top spot to
Protagoras; but as for being able to discuss a question, and
knowing how to defend, or test out, an idea, I'd be surprised if       c

he'd back off to anyone. So the way I see it, if Protagoras is admitting he isn't as good as Socrates at talking something through, then that's good enough for Socrates; but if he's still staking his claim, then he's got to carry on with the discussion, asking questions and giving replies – and he can't keep dragging out long speeches in response to every question, side-tracking the arguments, refusing to defend his ideas, and going on and

d  on until most people who are listening have forgotten what the question was about in the first place (not Socrates, mind you: I can guarantee that he won't forget, no matter what he says about being "a bit forgetful" – he's just messing with us.) So here's my view – because I think each of us should state clearly what he thinks about this: I say that Socrates is the one being more reasonable.'

After Alcibiades, I think it was Critias who spoke.

'Listen, Prodicus and Hippias; Callias here seems to me to be

e  very much on Protagoras' side; and Alcibiades is always very headstrong once he's launched himself into something. But there's no need for us to get involved and take sides with either Socrates or Protagoras. Instead I suggest we ask them both, from a neutral standpoint, not to break up the meeting when it's in full flow.'

337 a  When he'd said that, Prodicus said, 'Yes, I think that's quite right, Critias. People who find themselves present at these sorts of discussions certainly ought to be a *neutral* audience – although not, mind you, an *even-handed* one, which is not the same thing. They have to listen to both speakers neutrally, but they don't have to give an even hand to each man; rather, they should hand more to the more intelligent speaker and less to the less intelligent speaker. Now, personally, Protagoras and Socrates, I also feel you need to reach a compromise, and that in going over these ideas you should *debate* with one another

b  but not have a *dispute*. There's a difference: a debate is something that goes on even between friends, without ill feeling; a dispute, on the other hand, is what occurs between people who have fallen out with one another and are being hostile. And that way our meeting would proceed in the finest possible style. Because, in the first place, it would be the best way for you, as

the people speaking, to win the *respect* of those of us who are
listening. And I stress: our *respect*, not our *praise*. There's a
difference: respect is something that exists in the minds of the
audience, so it can't be phoney. Praise is just a matter of what
people say, and people often say the opposite of what they
really think. And secondly, it would be the best way of making   c
the meeting *enjoyable* for us, the people listening. And I stress:
*enjoyable*, not *pleasurable*. Enjoyment, you see, requires that
one be learning something, gaining some element of wisdom,
and is a purely mental experience; pleasure, on the other hand,
requires that one be eating something, say, or having some
other sort of pleasurable sensation, and is a purely physical
experience.'

That was what Prodicus had to say, and his comments were
well received by a lot of the people who were there. And after
Prodicus, it was Hippias, the famous intellectual, who spoke.

'Gentlemen,' he said, 'all of you who are here today: I look
upon you all as being of one family, true relatives, citizens of
one country – according to nature, that is; not according to
law. That's because, according to nature, if two things are   d
alike, then they belong to one family; but law, that tyrant of
humankind, often forces things on us in violation of our
nature.[58] So it would be a disgrace if we, of all people, in spite
of understanding the real nature of the world, and even though
we are the finest minds in Greece, and have come together by
virtue of that very status here in Athens, the world headquarters
of philosophy, and what's more, in this, the greatest and most
splendid household of that city – it would be a disgrace if we
failed to produce anything worthy of this prestigious occasion,   e
and instead just squabbled with one another as if we were a
bunch of utter good-for-nothings.

'So I'm asking you, Protagoras and Socrates, and I'm advising
you, to come to a middle ground, with us as the arbitrators, so
to speak, bringing you together – and that means you, Socrates,
mustn't insist on this very precise style of argument, where   338 a
everything is kept extremely brief, if that's something Protagoras doesn't enjoy; you should release, and relax, the reins of
your talk, to allow his speeches, for our benefit, to have a more

dignified, more handsome ring to them. And you, Protagoras, mustn't let out every cable to full stretch, unfurl your sail square to the wind and go tearing off into an open sea of speeches, beyond all sight of land. The two of you must strike a balance. So that's how I'd like you to do things – and I suggest you choose someone to act as an umpire, or moderator, or chair-
b man; someone to make sure both of you keep your contri-
butions to just the right length.'

These comments went down very well with the people there, and they all agreed it was a good idea. Callias said he wasn't going to let me leave, and they wanted to choose a moderator; at which point I said it would be insulting* to pick someone as a referee for the discussion. 'Because if the person who's chosen isn't as good as we are, well, it wouldn't make sense to have someone less good supervising people who are better than he is, while if he's just the same, that wouldn't make any sense either, since if he's just the same as us, he'll also *do* the same things we'd do anyway, so appointing him would be a waste of
c time. "So why not pick someone who's better than we are?" I hear you say. Well, in my view, it's impossible for you to pick someone who's genuinely smarter than Protagoras here. And if you go ahead and pick someone who isn't actually any better, and pretend that he is, that works out just as insulting to Protagoras – you'd be implying by your choice of moderator that he was just some ordinary guy. Of course, it wouldn't make any difference to *me*. I'm easy.

'Look, here's what I'm prepared to do to make it possible for us to carry on with the meeting and get some discussions going – which is what you're all so keen on: if Protagoras doesn't want
d to answer questions, fine, let's have him ask some questions, and I'll do the answering – and in the process I'll try to show him how I think someone who's answering questions should go about it. But then once I've answered as many questions as he feels like asking, he's got to answer my questions in the same way. And if, at that point, he doesn't seem very keen on giving answers that stick to the question, we'll all ask him together just the same thing as you're asking me – not to mess up the
e meeting. And there's no need for one particular person to be

supervisor just for that. You can all supervise the discussion together.'

Everyone thought that that was what we should do. So Protagoras, although he was very reluctant, found himself forced to go along with it: he would ask me some questions and then, once he'd had enough of asking questions, take his turn at answering mine – keeping his answers brief.

So he began asking his questions – something like this:

'I believe, Socrates,' he said, 'that a very important part of being a well-educated man is being a skilful critic of poetry. And by that I mean being able to see when the claims made by poets and songwriters make sense and when they don't, and knowing how to explain them* and defend your reading if you're asked questions about it. And in line with that, the question I'm going to ask now will still be about the same thing you and I have been talking about – being good – but shifted to a poetic context. That'll be the only change. Here it is:

'Simonides,[59] in one of his songs, says to Scopas, the son of Creon the Thessalian, that:

> Really and truly good
> is a hard thing
> for a man to become,
> I'll give you that –
> straight as a die,
> in hands and feet and mind,
> built without a single fault . . .

'Do you know the song? Or do you want me to go through the whole thing for you?'

'No, no need,' I said. 'I know the song – it so happens it's a song I've devoted quite a lot of thought to myself.'

'Excellent,' he said. 'In that case, do you think it's well put together and makes sense, or not?'

'Absolutely,' I said. 'I think it's very well put together and makes perfect sense.'

'But do you think it can count as being well put together if the poet contradicts himself?'

'No,' I said.

'Then you'd better take a closer look,' he said.

c    'No, really, Protagoras, I've looked it over pretty well already.'

'So you're aware, then, that later on in the song he says:

> But for me that Pittacus thing
> just don't quite ring –
> even though he is real smart –
> he says "bein' good is hard."

'You realize this is the same person who's making both claims, this one and the one before?'

'Yes, I'm aware of that,' I said.

'So do you think the second claim is consistent with the first one?'

'Yes, I think so' – at that moment, mind you, I was beginning to suspect he might be on to something. 'Why?' I said. 'You don't think so?'

d    'No! How could you possibly think someone who made both these claims was being consistent? Look, first of all, giving his own view, he claimed that it's hard to become a really good man, and then just a little bit further on in the song he forgot about that, and even though Pittacus is saying the same thing – that "bein' good is hard" – he criticizes him for it and says he can't accept his saying, even though it's just the same as his own! But by criticizing someone for saying the same thing as *he* does, obviously he's in effect criticizing *himself*. So that means that somewhere, either with the first claim or with the second, he's not making sense!'

Well, that got him a big round of applause from a lot of the

e    people in the audience. And as for me, at first I felt like I'd taken a punch from a champion boxer – everything went black! my head was in a spin! – with him making his point and then the rest of them heaping on the applause. But then – and between you and me the idea was to give myself a little time to think about what the poet might be saying – I turned and called to Prodicus.

'Prodicus,' I said, 'you're from Ceos – Simonides is your fellow countryman. It's your duty to come to the rescue! So I 340 a think I'm going to call on your support – just like the way, in the *Iliad*, the river Scamander calls to the Simoëis for help, when Achilles has him under siege – "Brother! Let's join our forces, to hold off the hero's might!" I'm calling on you for help, so we can stop Protagoras from reducing poor Simonides to rubble. And anyway, come to think of it, your special art form is exactly what's needed for making sense of the song, in Simonides' defence – the one which lets you explain the difference between *wanting* something and *desiring* something ("which is not the same thing") – and you gave us a number of b very fine examples of it just a moment ago. Here – see if you think the same way as me. Because I don't think Simonides is contradicting himself. Now let's hear your expert opinion first, Prodicus: do you think that *becoming* is the same thing as *being*, or different?'

'Different, of course!' said Prodicus.

'Right,' I said. 'Now, in the first quote, Simonides clearly stated his own view in his own words, which is that "it's a hard thing for a man to *become* really and truly good." Yes?'                c

'That's correct,' said Prodicus.

'And then he criticizes Pittacus,' I said, 'not – as Protagoras believes – for saying the same thing he does but for saying something quite different – because Pittacus didn't say *becoming* good was hard, which is what Simonides says; he said that "*bein'* good" is hard.[60] But being and becoming, Protagoras, aren't the same thing; not according to Prodicus here. And if being isn't the same thing as becoming, then Simonides isn't contradicting himself after all. And perhaps Prodicus here, along with lots of other people, would go along with Hesiod d when he says that, sure, *becoming* good is hard, because

> the gods laid it down,
> that a man's gotta sweat
> on the path to being good ...

but that once you

> reach the top, from then,
> hard as it was *to get there*,
> it's an easy thing
> to *keep a hold upon*.'

Prodicus, when he heard my idea, said he thought it was a good one. But not Protagoras: 'Your attempt to make sense of the song,' he said, 'involves a more serious problem than the one you're trying to make sense of.'

And I said, 'Oh no! What a disaster! Funny sort of doctor I am – I try to cure the illness, and I just make it worse!'

'I'm afraid so,' he said.

'Explain,' I said.

'The poet would have to be exceptionally stupid to claim that to *keep* being good is something so trivial, when in fact it's the most difficult thing there is. Everybody thinks so.'

Then I said, 'You know, it really is an amazing stroke of luck that Prodicus here happens to be sitting in on our discussion. Because I suspect, Protagoras, that Prodicus here possesses an inspired, and very ancient, branch of knowledge; and obviously Simonides was one of its earliest exponents – if not its founder. You apparently have no experience of this particular field (in spite of being an expert in *so* many others) – unlike myself: I'm an expert, thanks to being a student of Prodicus' here. And in this instance, I think that what you're not grasping is that maybe Simonides didn't take the word *hard* to mean the same thing as you take it to mean. It's like with the word *terribly*. Prodicus is always telling me off if I'm complimenting someone – you, for example – and I say, "That Protagoras, what a *terribly* clever guy". He asks me why I'm not embarrassed, calling *good* things *terribly* anything. "After all, something that's terrible," he says, "is bad. At any rate nobody ever says 'terrible money', 'terrible peace' or 'terrible health'; people talk about 'terrible disease' and 'terrible war' and 'terrible poverty', on the understanding that something terrible is something bad." So maybe it's the same with "hard". Maybe people in Ceos, including Simonides, take "hard" to mean "bad", or something else that you're not grasping. I know – let's ask

Prodicus. After all, he's the right person to ask about Simonides' dialect, isn't he? Prodicus, what exactly *did* Simonides mean by    c "hard"?'

'Bad,' he said.

'Aha! So that's also why he's criticizing Pittacus for saying that "bein' good is hard" – it's as if he took him to be saying that bein' good was something bad!'

'Well obviously, Socrates,' said Prodicus. 'What else did you think Simonides could be saying? He's clearly reprimanding Pittacus for not knowing how to make accurate semantic distinctions, because he's from Lesbos and was brought up speaking some barbarous dialect.'

'You hear that, Protagoras? You hear what Prodicus here is saying? What have you got to say to that?'                                 d

'That's nonsense, Prodicus,' said Protagoras. 'I'm quite certain Simonides meant the same thing by "hard" as the rest of us – not "bad" but something that isn't easy; something that takes a lot of trouble and effort.'

'Well, actually, Protagoras,' I said, 'that's what I think Simonides means, too; and I suspect Prodicus here knows full well that's what he means – if you ask me he's just messing with you, and testing to see if you'd be able to defend your claim. After all, it becomes perfectly obvious Simonides doesn't mean "bad" when he says "hard" with the very next thing he    e says – he says:

> only god could have that prize.

'Obviously he can't be saying that "bein' good" is something bad and the next moment say this is something "only god could have", and hand "that prize" exclusively to god! On that view, Prodicus would be making Simonides out to be some sort of scoundrel – not at all what we'd expect of a man from Ceos.

'Look, I'd be happy to tell you what I think Simonides is really getting at in the song – if you'd like to find out how I measure up as a "critic of poetry", as you put it – or I'll happily    342 a listen to what you have to say, if that's what you'd prefer.'

Protagoras, when he heard this suggestion, just said, 'Whatever you like, Socrates'. But Prodicus and Hippias absolutely insisted I go on, and so did everyone else.

'All right then,' I said. 'Let me try to explain to you what I think is going on in the song.

'The thing is, in all of Greece, people have been doing philosophy the longest, and studying it the most, in Crete and in
b Sparta,[61] and there are more sophists in those cities than anywhere else on earth. It's just that they claim not to have any interest in it and put on this big show of being morons – rather like the sophists Protagoras was talking about earlier – because they don't want anyone to figure out that it's really their philosophical expertise that gives them the upper hand over other Greeks. They want people to think that their superiority rests on fighting battles and being manly, because they reckon that if people realized what really gave them their edge – philosophy – then everyone would start trying to get good at it. As it is, by keeping it a closely guarded secret, they've completely fooled those people in the other cities who try to adopt "Spartan" customs. Those people, in their attempts to imitate the Spartans,
c go around bashing each other's ears and tying leather straps around their fists and doing lots of physical training and wearing little thigh-length coats – as if those are the things that make the Spartans the most powerful nation in Greece! The Spartans, meanwhile, when they feel like consulting their sophists without restriction, and are getting a bit sick and tired of meeting with them in secret, drive out all the foreigners, including the Spartophiles and any other foreigners who happen to be in town, and that way they can get together with their sophists without any outsiders finding out about it. And that's why* they don't allow
d any of their young men to travel to other cities (just like the Cretans) – to make sure they don't unlearn all the things they've taught them. And in these cities it isn't just the men who pride themselves on the quality of their education; the women are just the same.

'You'll see that what I'm saying is true – i.e. that Spartans really are given a superior education in philosophical discourse

– if you just think about the following: if anyone goes and has
a conversation with even the most mediocre Spartan, for most
of the discussion they'll find he comes across as someone pretty   e
ordinary, but then – at some unexpected point in the argument
– he'll fire in some really unforgettable quip, like some kind of
ace marksman, something dense and tightly packed – something
that makes the person he's talking to suddenly look no smarter
than a child.

'Now there are people around today who've noticed exactly
what I'm talking about, and there were also people who realized it in the past – i.e. that being Spartan is much more about
doing lots of philosophy than doing lots of physical training –
because they knew that the ability to produce those sorts of
pithy one-liners is the mark of a person of the highest intellec-   343 a
tual development. Thales from Miletus was one of these people,
and Pittacus from Mytilene, and Bias the Mysian, and our own
Solon, and Cleobulus from Lindos, and Myson from Chenae,
and the Spartan Chilon was spoken of as the seventh member
of the group.[62] All these people were imitators, admirers and
students of Spartan culture, and anyone can spot that that's the
style of their philosophy – tight, memorable maxims in every
case. And it was this same group who got together and presented the "first fruits" of their philosophy as an offering to    b
Apollo at his temple in Delphi; they inscribed those proverbs
everyone's always quoting: KNOW THYSELF and NOTHING
TOO MUCH.

'Why am I telling you all this? Well, to make the point that
this was the form philosophy took back in those early days –
a kind of Spartan-style pithiness. And a classic example was
this saying of Pittacus', which circulated privately and was
highly regarded by intellectuals: BEIN' GOOD IS HARD. Now
Simonides, who had philosophical pretensions of his own,      c
realized that if he could knock down this saying, like someone
knocking out a world-famous wrestler, and get the better of it,
he'd win that kind of fame himself among his contemporaries.
So the entire song is composed as a response to that particular
saying and for that purpose – as a deliberate ploy to knock it
off its perch. That's what I think.

'So let's all take a close look at the song together and see if what I'm saying is right.

'Now, straight off, the very first part of the song seems crazy, if he just wanted to say "it's hard to become a good man": if that was all he meant, why on earth would he have thrown in the
d phrase "I'll give you that"? There seems no point whatsoever in the phrase being thrown in, unless you take Simonides' words as forming a direct, hostile response to Pittacus' saying – i.e. Pittacus says:

BEIN' GOOD IS HARD

and Simonides, arguing against him, is saying "No! . . .

> Really and truly, good
> is a hard thing
> for a man to *become*,
> I'll give you that, [Pittacus]."

'He's not saying "really-and-truly-good"; that's not what he means the "really and truly" to go with – as if he thinks some
e people are really good while some people are good but . . . not really! That would clearly just be silly, and not something Simonides would ever say. No, we have to take the "really and truly" as going with the whole of what follows[63] – so that it's as if he'd just mentioned Pittacus' saying, just as if we had Pittacus himself making his claim, and then Simonides responding, with the one of them saying:

"Listen people, BEIN' GOOD IS HARD,"

and then the other responding:

344 a   "No, Pittacus, not right. *Being* good isn't hard. *Becoming* a good man (I'll give you that), straight as a die in hands and feet and mind, built without a single fault, that's what's hard, *really and truly*."

'That way, throwing in the "I'll give you that" seems to have some point to it, and likewise the "really and truly" (taken in the right way, as going with the whole sentence).[64] And everything that follows supports my interpretation. In fact, there are any number of things you could say about each and every line of the song to show just how well put together it is – the fact is, it's an extremely stylish, meticulously crafted piece. But it would take a long time to go through it in that kind of detail. Let's just run through its general outline and basic point, and show that it's definitely meant as a refutation of Pittacus' saying, from start to finish.

'Look at the next thing he says, just a few words further on: it's as if his argument went like this: that "*becoming* a good man is what's hard, really – though possible, at least, for a while – but having become a good man, to remain in that state – to *be* a good man (which is what you're talking about, Pittacus) – that's impossible,[65] and superhuman; the fact is,

> only god could have that prize;
> but a man, there *ain't no way*
> he can help bein' bad,
> when a real tough break
> beats every move he makes,
> and takes him down . . ."[66]

'All right, so, in the case of, say, sailing a ship, who is it that "a tough break that beats every move you make" can "take down"? Obviously not someone who knows nothing about sailing. Because he's just down for the count all along, isn't he? Now you can't knock someone over if they're already lying down. If someone's standing up, sure, then you can knock them over, thereby causing them to lie down; but not if they're lying down all along. Likewise, "a tough break that beats every move you make" could "take down" someone who's got plenty of moves but not someone who's got no moves to make in the first place – a captain, say, might be left with "no more moves to make" if he's caught by a heavy storm, a farmer might be

left "with no more moves" if he's hit by nasty weather, or a
doctor . . . you get the idea. The point is, someone who's good
is in a position to become bad – a view backed up by another
poet as well, the one who said that

> even a man who's good is sometimes bad,
> and sometimes good –

e   but someone who's bad is not in any position to *become* bad;
he's just bad all along, necessarily. So the claim is, "someone
who's got plenty of moves he can make – i.e. has knowledge
and is good – when a real tough break beats every move he
makes and takes him down, there *ain't no way* he can help
bein' bad. But you, Pittacus, you claim that "bein' good is
*hard*." Wrong. *Becoming* good is hard (I'll give you that) –
hard, but possible – bein' good, on the other hand, is *impossible*:

> 'Cause any man's good
> when he's doin' well;
> but any man who's doin' real bad,
> turns bad.[67]

345 a  'So, in the case of reading and writing, what counts as "doing
well" – what sort of "doing well" makes a person good at
reading and writing? Learning it, obviously. And what kind of
"doing well" makes someone a good doctor? Learning, obviously – learning how to look after patients. But if he's "doin'
real bad, he turns bad". So who, exactly, is in a position to
become a bad doctor? Clearly, someone who's (a) a doctor,
and (b) a good doctor. In that case, he's also in a position to
become a *bad* doctor. But as for those of us who know nothing
about medicine, there's no way that by "doing badly" we could
ever transform into doctors, or carpenters for that matter, or
b   anything else of the sort. And if you aren't in any position to
become a doctor by "doing badly", then it goes without saying
that you're in no position to become a *bad* doctor either. Likewise, a good *man* could also become a bad man, at some point,

either with the passing of time, or as a result of excessive strain
or illness, or through some other accident – remember, there's
only one thing that counts as "doing badly": losing your knowledge[68] – but a bad man can't *become* bad. He's bad to begin
with. If he's going to become bad, first he's got to become good.

'So it turns out this part of the song is driving at the same
point – that *being* a good man – i.e. permanently good – just   c
isn't possible, but it is possible to *become* a good man; and of
course that same person can also become bad. "And the people
who are the best the longest are the ones the gods love."[69]

'So all those claims are aimed at Pittacus; and the later lines
of the song make it even more obvious. He says:

> That's why I ain't gonna throw away
> the time I'm given,
> my dole of livin',
> on an empty hope,
> searchin' in vain for somethin' there *cannot be*:
> a man completely blame-and-blemish-free;
> at least, not among us mortal folks
> who earn our bread
> from the wide, wide land.
> (If I *do* find one, though,
> I'll let y'all know.)

'You can see how violently he's laying into Pittacus' saying at   d
every point of the song.[70]

> So long as he does no wrongin' wilfully
> I gonna give my praise
> and love to *any* man.
> Even the gods don't fight no battle
> against necessity.

'These lines are making exactly the same point. Simonides
wasn't so unsophisticated as to say he praises anyone who
doesn't *wilfully* do anything bad – as if he thinks anybody ever

*wilfully* does things that are bad! I mean, I pretty much think
e   that no one who knows anything believes that people ever make
mistakes wilfully or do things that are wrong, or bad for them,
wilfully. Smart people know full well that when you do things
that are wrong, or bad for you, you always do so without
meaning to. Simonides is no exception; he isn't saying he praises
anyone-who-doesn't-do-bad-things-wilfully;  he  means  the
"wilfully" to go with the "I'm going to give my praise."[71] He
was thinking, you see, that very often a decent man has to *force
himself* to be affectionate towards someone and praise them –
346 a   like, say, if his mother or father is cruel to him, or his country,
or something like that (it happens all the time). Nasty people
(he thought), when they get into a situation like that, are actually glad to see their parents' or their country's bad behaviour,
and they criticize it, and bring it to everyone's attention, and
denounce it – because then they can ignore their obligations
without being criticized themselves, without people reproach-
ing *them* for their neglect – and that means they criticize all the
b   more, and add on gratuitous reasons for quarrelling on top of
the ones we can't avoid. Good people, on the other hand, try
to be tactful and force themselves to find something nice to say,
and if they ever get angry with their parents or their country,
when they've been badly treated, they calm themselves down
and make up with them, by forcing themselves to show affection
to their own, and give them praise. Simonides likewise, I bet,
was thinking that plenty of times he'd praised or eulogized
some dictator, say, or someone like that, not out of choice but
out of "necessity".

c       'So this is what he's saying to Pittacus: "Listen, Pittacus, I'm
not criticizing you because I think criticizing people is *fun*; the
fact is, for me, it's good enough if a man's not bad; if he's

> . . . not too out-a-hand,
> and has the sense of right
> that does a city good – a solid guy.
> I ain't gonna pick no fault
> with a man like that . . .

"(because I'm not someone who enjoys finding fault with
people).

> After all, ain't there a limitless supply
> of dumbass fools?"

'He means, if you do enjoy criticizing people, you can criticize
*them* to your heart's content.

> The way I see it,
> anything's all right,
> if there ain't no shame in it.[72]

'He's not saying that as if he were saying "Anything's white if     d
there's no black in it" – because that would just be completely
absurd – no; he's saying that personally, he's prepared to accept
even the middle ground; that's enough for him not to criticize.
"I'm not looking for a man who's completely blame-and-
blemish-free," he said, "at least not among all us mortal folks
who earn our bread from the wide, wide land; if I do find one,
though, I'll let you know." He means, "If I was that fussy, I'd
never praise anyone at all! No, I'm happy if a man is averagely
good – i.e. as long as he doesn't *do* anything bad":

> so long as he *does* no wrongin'

'– and you've got to put a comma in here, right before the
"wilfully" –

>                                     , wilfully
> I gonna give my praise
> and love to any man

'(notice how here he's gone into Mytilenian slang – "*I gonna
give* my praise" – that's because he's speaking directly to
Pittacus). "There are people, on the other hand, that I praise
and love *against my will*. So if you'd been saying things that
were even half-way reasonable and true, Pittacus, there's no     347 a

way I'd be criticizing you. But as it is, since in fact you're
extremely wrong about things that are really important, and
yet people think that you're right – that's why I'm criticizing
you."

'So there you go, Prodicus and Protagoras,' I said. 'That's what
I think Simonides was meaning to say when he wrote the
song.'

And Hippias said, 'Well, I think that's a very fine explanation
b  of the song you've given us, Socrates. Having said that, it
happens I have a little theory about it of my own, a rather
nice one – which I'll be happy to explain to you all, if you're
interested . . .'

'Yeah, sure, Hippias,' said Alcibiades, 'only, some other time.
Right now what should happen is that Protagoras and Socrates
should do what they agreed to do – if Protagoras wants to ask
anything else, Socrates should provide answers; or if he's ready
to do the answering, Socrates should ask some questions.'

And I said, 'I'm happy to leave it up to Protagoras; whichever
he prefers. But if it's all right with him, let's not bother with any
more songs or poems – what I'd really like to do, Protagoras, is
c  go back to the things I asked you about at the start and come
to some conclusion by looking into them with your help. In
any case, I've always felt that discussions about poetry are
exactly like those parties thrown by low-class, vulgar people –
they do the same: they aren't capable of entertaining each other
over their drinks just with their own company, with the sound
of their own voices and their own ideas – because of their lack
of sophistication – so they drive up the price of flute-girls by
d  paying out a lot of money to get a "voice" in from somewhere
else – the sound of the flute – and then rely on that "voice" for
entertaining one another. But at parties where decent, classy
people are drinking together, educated people, you won't find
any flute-girls, or dancing-girls, or harp-girls. No. You'll find
they're quite capable of entertaining one another just with their
own company, without any of that kind of silly, adolescent
nonsense, relying on the sound of their own voices, taking turns
to speak and to listen to one another in an orderly fashion –

even if they drink a whole lot of wine. The same applies to  e
meetings like this one here: as long as the people taking part
are the sort of people most of us claim to be, then they shouldn't
need any outside voice, not even the voice of poets and songwriters – who can't be asked anything about what they're
saying, and usually when people bring them into a discussion
you get some people saying the poet means one thing and
others saying he means something else, when really they're
discussing something they have no way of proving one way or
the other. No, they don't bother with those sorts of discussions;
they just engage with one another through their own ideas,  348 a
making their own claims, and testing and defending them in
turn.

'Those are the kind of people I think you and I should try to
be more like; I think we should shelve the poets and make our
claims to one another on our own, through our own ideas,
investigating the real world and examining *ourselves*. So if you
want to ask some more questions, I'm prepared to go along
with that and do the answering; or, if you like, you could go
along with my idea of finishing off the things we were in the
middle of talking about when we broke off.'

Now, when I said that and other things along those lines,  b
Protagoras wouldn't give a straight answer as to which he'd
do. At which point Alcibiades looked over at Callias and said,
'What do you think now, Callias? Do you still think what
Protagoras is doing is fine? – refusing to state clearly whether
or not he'll let himself be questioned? Because I certainly don't
think so. I say he should either carry on with the discussion or
state once and for all that he refuses, and that way the rest of
us can know just where he stands, and Socrates, or for that
matter whoever else wants to, can talk to someone else.'

Protagoras, because he felt embarrassed (that's the feeling I  c
got, anyway) – embarrassed by Alcibiades' comments, and
because Callias and practically everyone there was asking him
to – eventually came round to the idea of going on with the
talk and told me to ask away; he'd answer my questions.

So I said, 'Listen, Protagoras, you mustn't think I'm talking
things through with you like this for any reason other than to

get to the bottom of certain things I'm constantly feeling baffled about myself. Because I think Homer was exactly right when he said,

d                    If two men go together, side by side,
                     one man may spy a thing before his friend . . .

'The fact is, we've got a much better chance of succeeding that way,* in whatever we're doing, or saying, or thinking about. That's true for all of us.

                     And if a man spies something on his own . . .

' . . . then he immediately goes around looking for someone to show it to, to get some kind of confirmation, and he keeps on looking until he finds someone. I'm the same; that's why I'm here talking to you, and that's why I'm happier talking about things with you than with anyone else at all; because I think you're likely to be the very best there is at looking into all the various things a decent man ought to think about – but especi-

e   ally the question of what it is to be good. Because let's face it, who could possibly be better at it than you? After all, you don't just think you're a good and decent man yourself . . . just as various others are pretty decent people themselves; but they can't make other people good, whereas in your case you're a good person yourself, and you can make other people good, and you've got so much belief in yourself that even though

349 a  everyone else in this profession keeps it a secret, you've come out and officially announced yourself to the whole of Greece, styled yourself a "sophist", promoted yourself as someone who teaches people about being good – the first person ever to feel he had the right to charge money for that sort of thing. So obviously I was bound to call on your help in looking into these things, and ask you questions, and seek your advice. How could I possibly not have?

    'And in this case I'd like to go back to my original questions. I want to start again from the beginning – get you to refresh my memory on one or two points, and then join you in looking into a couple more.

'I think the question went like this: "knowledge", "good b sense", "bravery", "respect for what's right" and "religiousness" – are these five terms all just different names for the same thing, or is there some separate entity underlying each of the terms, a thing with its own particular role, without any of them being like any other? Now you said that they weren't just different terms for one and the same thing, but that each of the terms had its own particular thing that it applied to, and that c they were all parts of being a good person – not in the same way as parts of gold, which are the same as one another, and the same as the whole chunk that they're the parts of, but in the same way as the parts of the face, which are different from the whole face that they're the parts of, and different from one another, and which all have their own special role. If that's what you still believe – the same as you did then – just say so. Or if you now think something slightly different, then just set out precisely what that is – I certainly won't hold it against you if you do say something different now. The fact is, I wouldn't be surprised if you were only saying that stuff earlier on because you wanted to see if I'd fall for it.' d

'No, listen, Socrates,' he said, 'what I'm saying is that these are all parts of being a good person, and that four of them are pretty closely related to one another, but that bravery is something very different from all the rest. And here's how you'll see that what I'm saying is right – you'll come across plenty of people who have no concern at all for what's right, are utterly disrespectful of religion, not remotely sensible and completely ignorant, and yet extremely and exceptionally brave.'

'Hold it there,' I said. 'What you're saying is well worth e looking into. When you say "brave people", do you mean people who aren't afraid of things? Or something else?'

'Yes, and people with guts; people who keep on going in the face of things most of us find frightening.'

'All right, next question: Do you think of being a good person as something honourable? Is it precisely because it's an honourable thing that you've set yourself up as someone who teaches it?'

'Well, of course!' he said. 'It's the most honourable thing there is – unless I'm losing my mind!'

'So is it that one or two elements of it are shameful and the rest honourable, or is every single bit of it honourable – the whole thing?'

'Every bit of it. The whole thing is about as honourable as anything gets.'

'All right, fine. So, do you know what sort of people aren't 350 a  afraid to dive down into wells?'

'Yes. Divers.'[73]

'And is that because they know what they're doing, or is there some other reason?'

'It's because they know what they're doing.'

'And what kind of people aren't afraid when it comes to fighting battles on horseback? Trained horsemen or people who can't ride?'

'Trained horsemen.'

'And what about when it comes to fighting with light arms? Trained light-armed fighters or people who aren't trained?'

'The trained fighters, and it's the same with everything else as well – if that's the general point you're after,' he said. 'People who know what they're doing feel less afraid than people who don't know what they're doing, and become less afraid than b  they were before when they gain the relevant knowledge.'

'But have you ever noticed people with no knowledge of any of these things who'll have a go at any one of them – without being afraid?'

'I certainly have – and they should be a lot more afraid than they are!'

'So people who are unafraid in that way – are they being brave?'

'No!' he said. 'That would make bravery something shameful. People like that are crazy!'[74]

'All right. So what is it you mean when you say "brave people"?' I said. 'Didn't you say they're people who aren't afraid?'

'Yes, and that's what I'm still saying,' he said.

'So, those people, the people who are unafraid in the way we c
just mentioned, aren't brave; it turns out they're just crazy.
Right? And then in the other cases it's people with the most
knowledge that are also the least afraid. And if they're the least
afraid, that means they're the bravest. Yes? So by that line of
reasoning it looks as if bravery is knowledge.'

'No, Socrates,' he said. 'No. You're not quite remembering what I said in my replies. You asked me if being brave
means not being afraid; and that's what I agreed to. You didn't
ask me if it's also the case that not being afraid means being
brave. Because if you had asked me that at the time, I'd have
said, "No, not in every case." As for the claim I did agree to, d
that brave people are people who aren't afraid of things – you
haven't shown me at any stage that I wasn't perfectly correct.
Then you go and point out that people with knowledge feel less
afraid than they did without their knowledge, and less afraid
than other people who don't have that knowledge, and you
think that shows that bravery and knowledge are the same
thing. But by that line of reasoning you could even persuade
yourself that physical strength was knowledge! Look – following exactly the same method, you could start off by asking me
if being physically strong means having ability; and I'd say
"Yes, it does." Then you'd ask if people who *know* how to e
wrestle have more *ability* at it than people who don't know
how to wrestle, and more ability when they learn how to do it
than they had before, and I'd say, "Yes, they do." And once
you'd got me to agree to that, you'd be in a position to use
exactly the same line of inference and claim that according to
my own admission physical strength *is* knowledge! But I'm at
no stage agreeing, here either, that people with any ability must
be physically strong – just that being strong gives people a
certain ability. The point is, ability and physical strength aren't 351 a
the same thing: one of them – ability – can also just be a result
of knowledge, or even arise from madness, or anger, while
strength comes from our nature, and from the proper conditioning of our bodies. It's the same in the other case. My point
is, a lack of fear is not the same thing as bravery. That's how it

comes about that, yes, being brave means not being afraid, but merely not being afraid doesn't always amount to being brave – because a lack of fear can also just be a result of know-how,

b   or anger, or madness – rather like ability – while bravery is something that comes from our nature, and from the proper conditioning of our souls.'

'Would you say, Protagoras,' I said, 'that some people's lives go well, and some people's lives go badly?'

'Of course.'

'So do you think a person's life could be said to be going well if they were living a life of pain and suffering?'

'No,' he said.

'What if they lived a pleasant life, right to the very end? Do you think in that case their life would have gone well?'

'Yes.'

c   'So in other words, to live a pleasant life is good, and to live an unpleasant life is bad?'

'Provided you live your life taking pleasure in the things that are honourable[75] – yes.'

'Oh? What do you mean by that, Protagoras? Not you too! Don't tell me you think the way most people do – that there are some pleasurable things that are bad and some painful things that are good? I mean, what I'm saying is, aren't things that are pleasurable good, just in so far as they're pleasurable, leaving aside whatever else might come out of them? And with things that are painful, likewise, aren't they bad to the extent that they're painful?'

'I don't know, Socrates; I don't know if I can give you an

d   answer that's as simple as the way you frame the question, and just say that all pleasurable things are good and all painful things are bad. It seems to me that it would be safer for me to say – not just with a view to getting the answer right, but also if I look back over the whole of my life – that there are some pleasurable things that aren't good and some painful things that aren't bad; and there are some that are; and there's a third class that aren't either good or bad.'

'By "pleasurable things",' I said, 'do you mean things that involve or bring about pleasure?'

'Absolutely,' he said.                                                         e

'Well, look; here's what I'm saying: aren't they good at least in so far as they're pleasurable? In effect, I'm asking if pleasure just considered on its own is a good thing.'

'Well, as you're so fond of saying, Socrates,' he said, '*let's look into it*, and if the idea seems to make sense when we look into it, and "pleasurable" turns out to be the same thing as "good", we'll agree; and if not, that'll be the time to disagree.'

'So would you like to lead the inquiry,' I said, 'or do you want me to?'

'You should take the lead,' he said. 'You're the one introducing the idea.'

'In that case,' I said, 'I wonder if this might be a way for us    352 a
to get to the bottom of things: imagine you were giving someone a check-up, trying to get some idea of their health, or some bodily function, just from their appearance, and you'd had a look at their face and their hands, and then said, "Come on then, take off your shirt and show me your chest and your back as well, so I can get a better look at you." I need to do something a bit like that as well, for the purposes of our investigation. I've had a look and seen that your attitude to what's good and what's pleasurable is as you say, and now I feel like saying something like this: All right then, Protagoras, time to uncover another aspect of your way of thinking . . . what's your attitude    b
to knowledge? Do you feel the same way as most people about that as well, or do you take a different view? Now what most people think about knowledge is something like this: that it isn't something powerful, or something that governs us or controls us – they don't think of it as being that sort of thing at all. They think that often, even though there's knowledge in a person, it isn't their knowledge that controls them but something else – sometimes anger, sometimes pleasure or pain; sometimes love and often fear – as if knowledge were a slave – that's exactly how they think of it – being pushed and shoved around    c
by everything else. So do you think something like that as well?

Or do you think knowledge is something noble, and that it's in its nature to govern us, and that if someone knows what's good and what's bad, nothing can overpower them and force them into doing something other than what their knowledge is telling them to do – that a man's wisdom always has the power to save him?'

d    'Yes, Socrates; not only is that what I believe,' he said, 'but what's more, considering who I am, it would be disgraceful if I didn't think of knowledge and wisdom as the most powerful and important forces in the whole sphere of human life.'

'Well, I'm pleased to hear you say that,' I said, 'and you're right. So you realize most people don't agree with you and me on this one? They think often people know what's best for them and still don't want to do it, even though they could – they do something else instead. Now I've asked lots of people what on earth could be the explanation for this, and they all tell me that people who behave that way do it because they "can't resist the

e    pleasure", or "can't stand the pain", or are "overpowered" by one of those other things I was talking about a second ago.'

'Well, presumably people say lots of other things that are wrong as well, Socrates.'

'Well, come on then, help me try and persuade these people, explain to them what's really happening to them when they

353 a    say, "We can't resist the pleasure, and that's why we're not doing what's best for us; because we certainly *know* what's best." Because if we said to them, "No, that's not right, you people; you've got it all wrong," they'd probably say, "All right, Protagoras and Socrates, if what's happening here isn't a matter of not being able to resist pleasures, then what on earth is it? What do you say it is? Go on, tell us!"

'But why do we have to look at what ordinary people think, Socrates? Most people just say the first thing that comes into their heads.'

b    'I think this may be of some use to us for finding out about bravery – how it relates to the other parts of being a good person. So if you're prepared to stick to what we decided just a moment ago – i.e. that I should take the lead in the way I think is going to be the best at making things clear, then follow along. Of course, if you don't want to – if it's what you'd prefer, we can just forget it.'

'No, no, you're right,' he said. 'Carry on as you started.'

'All right,' I said, 'start again. Suppose they asked us: "So c what do you say this is – the thing we call not being able to resist pleasures?" I'd say something like this to them: "All right, listen. Protagoras and I are going to try to explain.

'"Now I take it you people are saying this is something that happens to you in situations like these: often, say, you find you 'can't resist' certain kinds of food, or drink, or sex – things that are pleasurable – and even though you know they're bad for you, you go and do them anyway. Right?" They'd say yes; at which point you and I would come back at them with this: "But what exactly is it about these things that makes you say they're bad for you? Is it the fact that they give you that pleasure d at that moment; the fact that each of them is pleasurable? Or is it the fact that, in the long term, they make you ill, or make you poor, or bring about lots of other things like that? Or is the idea that even if they didn't bring about any of those things later on, even if their only effect was pure enjoyment, they'd still be bad for you – entirely regardless of the way they cause that enjoyment, whatever the details?" We can be pretty sure, can't we, Protagoras, that their reply would have to be that these things aren't bad for them because of the pleasure itself, just because they produce pleasure at that moment, but because of the things that happen later – being ill and so on?'                    e

'Yes, I think that's what most people would say,' said Protagoras.

'"And isn't the point that by making you ill, they're causing pain; and by making you poor, they're causing pain?" I think they'd agree.'

Protagoras thought so too.

'"So isn't it clear to you people – and this is what Protagoras and I are saying – that the only reason these things are bad for you is because they end up causing pain or make you miss out on other pleasures?" Would they agree?'                                         354 a

We both thought they would.

'All right. Now suppose we go back and ask them the

opposite question: "You people who say some good things are painful: I take it you mean things like physical training, and doing military service, and being treated by doctors when the treatment involves burning, and slicing, and drugs, and starvation diets? You're saying those things are good for you but painful?" Would they say that was right?'

He thought so.

b    ' "So, why exactly do you say they're good? Is it the very fact that they produce, at that moment, total agony and excruciating pain? Or is it because they give rise, in the long term, to things like health, and good physical condition, and national security, and power over other countries, and wealth?"[76] They'd say it was the latter, I suspect.'

He thought so too.

' "But are those things good for any reason besides the fact that they end up producing pleasures, and freeing you from pain, or helping you avoid pain? Or can you come up with

c    some other goal, something you have in mind when you call them 'good', that isn't to do with pleasures and pains?" I think they'd say they couldn't.'

'Yes, I think so too,' said Protagoras.

' "So in other words, you pursue pleasure as what's good, and avoid pain as what's bad?" '

He thought they'd go along with that.

' "So in fact, that's your notion of what's bad: pain. And your notion of what's good: pleasure. Because even when you call an experience of pleasure 'in itself' something bad, it's only when it's making you miss out on pleasures greater than the ones it contains itself, or bringing about pains greater than the

d    pleasures you're getting from that experience. Because if there's any other sense in which you ever call experiencing pleasure something bad 'in itself', if you've got any other goal in mind, you'd also be able to tell us what that is – but no, you won't be able to." '

'No, I don't think they will either,' said Protagoras.

' "And I take it it's the same story with experiencing pain – you only call experiencing pain something good 'in itself' when it's helping you avoid pains that are greater than the ones it

involves itself, or bringing about pleasures that are greater than
those pains? Because if you've got any other goal in mind when
you call being in pain something good 'in itself', anything other
than what I'm saying you have in mind, then you could tell us   e
what that is – but no, you won't be able to."'

'Yes. That's quite right,' said Protagoras.

'"All right then, you people, suppose your come-back was
to ask me this: 'So what on earth is the point of all this? Why
are you going on and on about it, in all this detail?' 'I'm sorry,'
I'd say. 'Just bear with me. Look, in the first place, it's no easy
task, showing what this thing you call "not being able to resist
pleasures" really is; and secondly, my entire argument hangs
on this particular point. But listen; even at this stage you've still
got the option of taking back what you've said, if you can come
up with anything else at all you can say is good besides pleasure,   355 a
or anything you can say is bad besides pain. Or is that all you
people want? – to live out your lives pleasurably, free from
pain? If that's all you want from life, and you can't come up
with anything else at all you can say is good or bad that doesn't,
in the end, come down to pleasure and pain, then get ready for
what follows. Because I'm telling you, if all of that is really the
case, then your claim turns out to be ridiculous – the claim that
often people know that certain things are bad for them yet do
them anyway, even though they don't have to, because they're
driven, and deranged, by pleasures; and the converse, that a   b
person can know what's good for them and yet refuse to do it,
because they can't resist pleasures on offer right here and now.'

'"We can make it perfectly clear that these claims are ridiculous if we stop using all the various names at the same time –
'pleasurable', 'painful', 'good' and 'bad' – and instead, since
they've turned out to be just two things, also start referring to
them by just two names: first let's use 'good' and 'bad', then
we'll switch and use 'pleasurable' and 'painful'. So now that
that's settled, let's try out the claim:   c

[1] Here's a person doing things that are bad for him, even
though he knows they're bad for him. So then someone asks:
Why?

'Because he can't resist,' we'll say.

'Can't resist what?' he'll ask. But we're not allowed to say, 'Can't resist the pleasure' any more, because now it's called something else; it's switched its name from 'pleasure' to 'what's good'. So let's answer the man, let's say, 'Because he can't resist . . .'

'Because he can't resist *what*?' he'll say.

'Because he can't resist what's good!' we'll say.

'Now suppose the man who's asked us the questions is a bit of a lout; he'll just laugh at us: "That's the silliest damn thing I ever heard! So he's doing things that are bad even though he knows they're bad, and even though he doesn't have to, because *he can't resist things that are good*? And these good things" (he'll say) "aren't worth it, right?* They don't outweigh the bad? Or are they worth it?"[77]

'Obviously our answer will have to be: "No, they're not worth it. Because if they were, then our man 'not resisting the pleasure' wouldn't be *making a mistake*."[78]

' "But what is it," he'll probably say next, "that makes good things 'not worth' bad ones, or bad things 'not worth' good ones? Surely it's simply a matter of one lot being bigger and the other lot smaller, or of there being more of one lot and less of the other?"

'We'll have to agree. What else can we say?

' "Well obviously then," he'll say, "what you actually mean by this 'not being able to resist' business is this: taking on a greater amount of bad just to get a smaller amount of good!"[79]

'All right, so now let's go back and switch the names for these same things to "pleasurable" and "painful", and say:

[11] Here's someone doing things that are – before, we said 'bad for him', but now we're saying 'painful' – he's doing things that are painful, even though he knows they're painful, *because he can't resist the pleasures*! – pleasures that obviously aren't worth it – i.e. that don't outweigh the pains.[80]

'But what other way is there for pleasures to be "not worth" pains (or *vice versa*), besides their exceeding or falling short of one another? And that's just a question of their being bigger or smaller than one another, or of there being more of one and fewer of the other, or of one lot being more painful or more pleasurable, and so on. Of course, somebody might say, "No, hold on, Socrates; there's a big difference between what's pleasurable here and now, and what's pleasurable or painful in the long term." "Maybe so," I'd say, "but surely no difference that isn't itself a matter of pleasure and pain. The fact is, there's no other way for them to differ. No, you've just got to be a kind of expert at weighing things up; you've got to put together all the pleasures, and put together all the pains (placing both kinds, short- and long-term, on the scales) and then say which lot there are more of. What I mean is, if you're weighing pleasures against pleasures, then you've always got to go for the ones that are bigger and that there are more of. And if you're weighing pains against pains, you've got to go for the ones that are smaller and that there are less of. And if you're weighing up pleasures against pains, then if it turns out that the pleasures outweigh the pains (whether it's pleasures that are a long way off outweighing short-term pains, or long-term pains being outweighed by present pleasures), that's what you should do, the action that involves those pleasures; whereas if the pains outweigh the pleasures, then that's something you shouldn't do. Isn't that right, people? Surely that's the way it is?" I'm certain there's no way they could possibly disagree.'

Protagoras thought so too.

'"Right then; given that that's the case, here's another question for you," I'll say. "When you're relying on your eyesight, objects of the same size seem bigger from up close and smaller from far away, don't they?" They'll agree. "And isn't it the same with thicknesses, and quantities? And sounds: don't sounds of equal volume seem louder from up close and fainter from far away?" They'd say, "Yes." "Right; so now imagine that doing well in life crucially depended on our ability to choose and 'do' large sizes, and avoid and not 'do' small sizes. What would have turned out to be the thing that saved us from disaster?

b

c

d

Would it be knowing how to measure things? Or the power of the way things appear? Think – wouldn't appearances mislead us* and have us rushing madly back and forth, constantly choosing and then rejecting the very same things, regretting our actions and choices – our selections of big things and little things? Measuring know-how, on the other hand, would cancel
e out the effect of those appearances; it would show us the truth, allow a person's soul to remain calm, and settled, and fixed on reality – it would save our lives. Wouldn't it?" Do you think our people would agree that, in that scenario, it would be measuring-know-how that would prove to be our salvation – or some other kind of know-how?'

He agreed. 'Yes, measuring-know-how.'

' "And what if our lives crucially depended on choosing from among odd and even numbers – a matter of knowing when we should choose larger numbers and when we should choose smaller numbers, whether we were comparing odd with odd, or even with even, or even with odd, whether the numbers were close to hand or a long way off? What would save us? Wouldn't
357 a it be knowledge? And wouldn't it be some form of knowledge of measurement, since it's to do with things exceeding or falling short of one another? And since it's odd and even numbers we're talking about, wouldn't it have to be knowledge of arithmetic?" Would our people agree with us on that or not?'

Protagoras, like me, thought they'd agree.

' "All right, people, so given that in the real world our lives have turned out to depend, crucially, on our correctly choosing pleasure and pain, greater and lesser amounts of them, bigger
b and smaller pleasures and pains, long-term and short-term, isn't it clear that what we desperately need is, for a start, some kind of measuring ability – since it's a matter of figuring out whether given pleasures and pains exceed, or match, or fall short of one another?" '

'Yes, that must be right.'

' "And if it's a kind of measuring, then presumably it has to be some form of know-how and knowledge?" '

'Yes, they'll go along with that.'

' "Right; now what kind of knowledge this would be, or what

kind of know-how, is something we can look into some other
time. The main thing is, it's knowledge, and that's all that's
needed for what Protagoras and I are supposed to be proving
to you people, in answer to your earlier question. You asked    c
your question – remember? – when the two of us agreed that
nothing was more powerful than knowledge, and that whenever
a person has knowledge it always overpowers pleasure and
anything else. So then you claimed that, no, plenty of times
even someone with knowledge 'can't resist pleasure' – and when
we disagreed with you, that was when you asked your question:
'All right, Protagoras and Socrates, if what's happening to
people in these situations isn't a matter of not being able to
resist pleasure, then what on earth is it? What do you say it is?
Go on, tell us!' Now if we'd said to you right there and then it    d
was just a matter of ignorance, you'd have laughed at us. But
you'd better not laugh now! Because if you do, you'll be laughing at yourselves as well! Because, look: you've now agreed,
yourselves, that when people make mistakes in choosing pleasures and pains – i.e. what's good for them or bad for them –
they make those mistakes through a lack of knowledge, and
not just any knowledge but specifically, as you also agreed just
a second ago, knowledge of measurement. But if somebody
makes a mistake through a lack of knowledge, presumably you
don't need me to tell you that the cause of that mistake is    e
*ignorance*. So it follows that that's what your 'not being able
to resist pleasure' really is – ignorance of the most serious kind.
And that's exactly what Protagoras here says he can cure for
you, and Prodicus, and Hippias. But you people, because you
think it's something other than ignorance, don't come to these
sophists yourselves (the people who can teach you all about
these things), and you don't send your children along to them
either – you assume this is something that can't be taught.
You'd rather keep your precious cash; so you don't give a penny
to these men here – and that's why you're all such failures, as
a society and in your personal lives!"

'There you go; that's how we'd have responded to the major-    358 a
ity of people. But now I'm asking you, Hippias and Prodicus,
along with Protagoras – I want you two to take part in the

discussion as well – what do *you* think? Do you think what I've been saying is right or wrong?'[81]

They were all overwhelmingly of the view that everything I'd said was true.

'So you mean you agree,' I said, 'that what's pleasurable is good and what's painful is bad? And I'll have to ask Prodicus here to spare me his precise semantic distinctions – I mean, whether you say "pleasurable", or "enjoyable", or "fun", or however or whatever you like calling these things, Prodicus,
b   my friend, you know what I'm getting at: just answer me focusing on that.'

Prodicus chuckled and said that he agreed, and so did all the rest of them.

'In that case, all of you,' I said, 'what about this? Actions that get us to that goal – to a life free from pain, a pleasurable life – aren't all such actions *honourable*?[82] Is an honourable action one that benefits us and is good for us?'

They thought that was right.

'So, if it's the case,' I said, 'that *pleasurable = good*, it follows that nobody can either know or believe that some alternative is better for them than what they're doing, and open to them,
c   and yet still do what they're doing, when they could be doing what would be better for them – and this "not being able to resist" business is really nothing but ignorance, and "self-control" is just a matter of knowledge.'

They all agreed.

'All right, how about this then: by "ignorance" you mean having beliefs that are false and being mistaken about things that are really important.'

They all agreed to that as well.

'So what we're saying, then,' I said, 'is that nobody ever willingly goes towards things that are bad for them, or even things they think are bad for them – it turns out that's an
d   impossibility of human nature; to go towards things you believe are bad for you, willingly, instead of what you think is good; and nobody, if they're forced to choose between two things that are both bad for them, could ever choose the bigger bad

thing if they're in a position to choose the smaller bad thing. Yes?'

We all agreed that all of that was right.

'All right then, next question,' I said. '"Being afraid" or "being scared" – do you take it to be the same thing as I do? This is one for you, Prodicus. Whichever you call it – "being afraid" or "being scared" – I take it to be this: believing that something bad is going to happen to you.'

Protagoras and Hippias thought that that was what both "being afraid" and "being scared" amounted to; Prodicus thought that that was what "being afraid" was, but that "being scared" was different.                                                           e

'Well, you know what, Prodicus,' I said, 'it doesn't really matter. The point is this. If what we've said so far is right, the question is, is anyone ever going to go towards things they're afraid of, willingly, if they've got the option of going towards things they're *not* afraid of? Or does what we've agreed make that impossible? Because things you're afraid of, we've just agreed, are things you believe are bad for you; and we agreed that nobody ever goes towards – i.e. willingly chooses – things they think are bad for them.'

They all thought that was right as well.                           359 a

'All right; so now that we've established all of that, Prodicus and Hippias, I want Protagoras here to explain to us how the answer he gave back at the start can be right – not the answer he gave right at the very start; back then he said there were five parts of being good, and none of the five was like any other, and each had its own special role. That's not what I mean. I mean what he said a bit later on. Later on he said four of the five were pretty closely related to one another, but one of them, bravery, was very different from all the rest, and that I'd see   b that that was the case "from the following bit of evidence", he said: "You'll come across people, Socrates, who've got no respect whatsoever for religion, who don't care at all about what's right, who aren't remotely sensible, and who're extremely ignorant – yet exceptionally brave. That shows bravery is something totally different from the other parts of being good." And at the time I was very surprised at his reply;

that was my instant reaction; and I'm even more surprised now
that I've run through these various arguments with you people.
At any rate, I asked him if by brave people he meant people
who aren't afraid of things, and he said, "Yes, and people

c  who can keep on going."[83] Do you remember saying that,
Protagoras?'

He said he did.

'All right then,' I said. 'In that case I want you to tell us what
it is that brave people "keep on going" *towards*? The same
things as cowards?'

'No,' he said.

'So towards different kinds of things then?'

'Yes.'

'Is it that cowards only go towards things that aren't frightening, while brave people go towards things that *are* frightening?'

'That's certainly what people say, Socrates.'

'You're quite right,' I said, 'that is what people say. But that's

d  not what I'm asking you. I'm asking you what *you* say brave
people go towards. Things that are frightening, believing them
to be frightening, rather than* things that *aren't* frightening?'

'Well, no, that can't be right,' he said. 'That was shown
by your line of reasoning to be impossible – just a moment
ago.'

'You're right again!' I said. 'So assuming that argument was
correct, in fact nobody ever moves towards the things they
believe are frightening (because "lacking self-control" turned
out to be just a case of ignorance).'[84]

He agreed.

'And of course, everybody goes towards the things they're
*not* afraid of, cowards and brave people alike; and in that

e  sense, at least, cowards and brave people go towards the same
things.'

'But that's simply not the case, Socrates!' he said. 'There's a
world of difference between what cowards and brave people go
towards! I mean, take war for example; brave people are prepared to go into battle, and cowards refuse.'

'And is going into battle,' I said, 'honourable or shameful?'

'Honourable,' he said.

'And if it's honourable, then by what we agreed earlier on it must be good for them. Remember, we agreed that *all honourable actions are good for us.*'[85]

'That's true; we did. And that's what I still think now.'

'And you're quite right,' I said. 'So which kind of people is it you say refuse to go into battle, even though it's the honourable thing to do, and therefore good for them?'   360 a

'Cowards,' he said.

'And if it's the honourable thing to do, and good for them, it must also be pleasurable, yes?'

'Well, that's certainly what we agreed,' he said.

'So when cowards refuse to go towards what's more honourable, and so better for them, and so more pleasurable, are they aware that that's what they're doing?'

'Well, no. If we accept that,' he said, 'we'll be messing up our earlier findings.'

'And what about brave people? They go towards what's more honourable, and better for them, and more pleasurable, yes?'

'Yes.' He said. 'I'm forced to agree.'

'Now as a general rule, with brave people, there's no shame in their being afraid of what they're afraid of (when they *are*   b afraid of something);[86] and there's no shame in their *not* being afraid of the things they're *not* afraid of. Right?'

'Yes, that's right,' he said.

'And if there's shame in it, then it's honourable?'

He agreed.

'And if it's honourable, that means it's also good for them?'

'Yes.'

'But with cowards, or people who are reckless or crazy, it's the reverse: when they're afraid of things, their fear is shameful, and when they're *not* afraid of things, their *lack* of fear is shameful.'[87]

He agreed.

'But how can they be unafraid of things that are shameful, and therefore bad for them? It must be through just not realizing – a result of ignorance?'[88]

'Yes, that's right,' he said.

c     'All right, so tell me, what do you call the thing that causes cowards to be cowards? Cowardice or courage?'

'Cowardice, of course.'

'And it turns out cowards are cowards because of their ignorance of what's really frightening?'

'Yes, absolutely,' he said.

'So in other words, that ignorance is what causes them to be cowards?'

'Yes.'

'And you're agreeing that *cowardice* is what causes people to be cowards?'

'Yes, I am.'

'So it looks as if cowardice just *is* ignorance of what you should and shouldn't be afraid of?'

He nodded.

'And of course, bravery is the opposite of cowardice?'

'Yes.'

d     'And isn't knowledge of what you should and shouldn't be afraid of the opposite of ignorance of what you should and shouldn't be afraid of?'

Here again he still nodded.

'And ignorance of those things is what cowardice is?'

This time his nod was rather slow in coming.

'So that means that bravery is . . . *knowledge* – i.e. a matter of knowing what you should and shouldn't be afraid of, since that's the opposite of *not* knowing what you should and shouldn't be afraid of. Right?'

By this point he wasn't any longer prepared even to give a nod; he just sat there in silence. So I said, 'What's the matter, Protagoras? Can't answer the question? Even with a plain yes or no?'

'You can finish it off yourself,' he said.

'All right,' I said, 'as long as I can ask just one more thing –

e     whether you still believe, as you did at the start, that there are some people who are "extremely ignorant but exceptionally brave"?'

'You don't let up, do you, Socrates? You seem dead set on

making me answer all the questions! Well, all right, I'll say it, if it makes you happy: No. In the light of all the things that we've agreed, I now believe that that's impossible.'

'You really mustn't think,' I said, 'that I have any aim in asking you all these questions beyond a simple desire to investigate; to investigate all aspects of being good, especially what on earth being good exactly is. And that's because I'm sure that getting clear on that would be the best way to get to the bottom of the 361 a problem you and I have had this long, drawn-out discussion over – whether or not being good is something people can be taught – with me claiming it isn't and you claiming it is.

'And, if you ask me, the point we've ended up at in our discussion is like a person scolding us and laughing at us; and if our Ending could somehow speak to us, she'd be saying, "Protagoras and Socrates! You two guys are so silly! You, Socrates, earlier on, were claiming that you can't make people good by teaching them, and now you're determined to contradict yourself. You're trying to prove that everything – doing   b what's right, being sensible, being brave – the whole lot of them – that they're all just a matter of knowledge; which is exactly the way to make it seem that being good *is* something you can be taught. (After all, if being good were something other than a kind of knowledge, the claim Protagoras is trying to argue for, then obviously it wouldn't be something teachable. But if it's really going to turn out to be entirely a matter of knowledge, the line you're pushing for, Socrates, it'll be totally amazing if it can't be taught.) And you, Protagoras, you started off by claiming it could be taught, and now you're saying the complete opposite; you seem desperate for it to turn out to be practically *anything but* knowledge, which is just the way to make it look   c as unteachable as possible."

'Now, personally, Protagoras, when I realize that everything's going all topsy-turvy like this and winding up in this hopeless mess, I find myself really anxious to get to the bottom of it all; and I'd very much like for us to run through these questions carefully, come to some understanding of exactly what it is to be a good person, and then go back and have

another go at figuring out whether or not it's something that can be taught – otherwise I'm worried our old friend Thinxtoo-
d  late may just go on and on duping us, and tripping us up in our investigations – just as he forgot about us, according to you, when he was handing things out. Now I liked Thinxahead much more than Thinxtoolate in your story; and it's because I'm using him as my role-model and trying to think ahead, carefully, about the whole future course of my life that I take so much trouble over these things – and if you'd like to, as I said back at the start, it would be a real pleasure to have a thorough look into these things with you. You more than anyone.'

And Protagoras said, 'Well, Socrates, I'd like to say that I really admire your enthusiasm and the way you've taken us through your arguments: I reckon I'm not a bad sort of a man, generally speaking, and I'm certainly the last person in the
e  world to be ungracious. As a matter of fact, I've spoken about you to lots of people. I've often said that you're by far the most impressive man I've met – at any rate, certainly the most impressive of your generation. And I can say here and now that I wouldn't be surprised if you ended up as a pretty famous name in philosophy.

'As for these questions – we'll go through them some other time; whenever suits you best. But now I think it's about time we turned to something else.'

362 a  'Well, if that's your decision, then I suppose I have no choice,' I said. 'In any case there's somewhere I was supposed to go, a long while back. I only stayed as a special favour to Callias, since he's so beautiful.'

Well, there you go. That's what was said, by us and by them. That's when we left.

# MENO

*or*
*On Being Good*

# Characters

SOCRATES, *a philosopher (here aged about sixty-seven)*
MENO, *a young aristocrat from Thessaly*
SLAVE, *one of Meno's slaves*
ANYTUS, *an Athenian politician; Meno's host in Athens*

*The dialogue is set in Athens, in about 402 BC, a few years after the city's final defeat in the Peloponnesian War, and just after the restoration of the democracy following the dictatorship of the Thirty Tyrants. Two years later, Meno was killed while fighting as a mercenary in Persia; shortly after that, in 399 BC, Socrates was put on trial on suspicion of promoting anti-religious views and corrupting the young, and was executed. Anytus was one of the prosecutors.*

MENO: Can you tell me, Socrates – is *being good* something    70 a
you can be taught?[1] Or does it come with practice rather
than being teachable? Or is it something that doesn't come
with practice *or* learning; does it just come to people naturally? Or some other way?

SOCRATES: In the old days, Meno, you Thessalians were known
and admired all over Greece for horsemanship and wealth.
But times have changed: it seems these days you're also    b
known for being intellectuals – especially if you're from Larissa, like your mate Aristippus.[2] And the man you can thank
for that is Gorgias:[3] he's come to town and won over the top
men in Larissa's ruling family as his intellectual fans – they're
crazy about him (including Aristippus, who's crazy about
*you*), and so are the rest of Thessaly's elite. For one thing,
he's got you into this habit of giving answers – confidently
and generously – to any question anyone ever asks you, just
as you'd expect from people with knowledge. Because that's
his thing: he likes to challenge all comers, all over Greece, to    c
ask him any question they want, and he never, ever fails to
have an answer. But here in Athens, Meno, the situation is
exactly the reverse. There's been a kind of intellectual
drought. It looks to me like knowledge has left this part of    71 a
the world and moved to Thessaly. At any rate if you try
asking anyone round here a question like that, they'll just
laugh in your face. 'Stranger!' they'll say, 'you seem to take
me for a very fortunate man! At any rate, you seem to think
I might know whether being good is something you can be
taught, or how exactly people become good, when the fact

is, so far from knowing whether or not it's teachable, I
haven't even got the faintest idea what being good *is*!' Well,
b    that's just how it is with me too, Meno. This is one area
where I'm just as hard up as my fellow Athenians, and I'm
the first to admit that I haven't got the faintest idea what
*being good* is. And if I don't know *what* it is, how on earth
am I supposed to know *what kind* of thing it is? Or do you
think that's possible? Do you think that if someone has no
idea who Meno is, they can know if Meno's beautiful, or if
he's rich, or if he's from a good family, or the opposite of all
those things? Does that seem possible to you?

MENO: No, I suppose not. But come on, Socrates; do you really
c    not even know what being good *is*? Is that what you want us
to say about you to people back home?

SOCRATES: That's not all. You can also tell them that I've
never met anyone else who knows, either – or I don't think
I have.

MENO: Really? Didn't you meet Gorgias when he was here?

SOCRATES: Yes, I did.

MENO: So, didn't you think he knew?

SOCRATES: My memory isn't all that good, Meno. So I couldn't
tell you right now exactly what I thought at the time . . . But,
yes, maybe he does know . . . and you probably know what
he said. So why don't you just remind me? Or, if it's all right
d    with you, tell me what you think yourself – presumably you
think the same as he does?

MENO: That's right, I do.

SOCRATES: Well, in that case forget Gorgias. He isn't here, is
he? Let's hear what you have to say, Meno: what do you
think being good is, for heaven's sake? Don't be stingy. Let's
hear it. Show me that what I've just said isn't true – I'll never
have felt so lucky I was wrong, if it turns out you and Gorgias
know the answer, when I've just said I've never met a single
man who knew.

e    MENO: Well, it's not very difficult, Socrates. First, if you want
to know what being good is *for a man* – well, that's easy.
Here's what being a good man is: having what it takes to
handle your city's affairs, and, in doing so, to help out your

friends and hurt your enemies[4] (while making sure they don't do the same to you). Or, if you want me to explain what being a good *woman* is, no problem: she's got to be good at looking after the home, be thrifty with household goods and always obey her man. And then there's being a good child (a boy or a girl) or being a good old man (free, if you want, or, if you like, a slave) – and there are all sorts of other cases of being good. So there's no need to feel baffled about what being good *is*! The thing about 'being good' is that it's different for each of us; it varies according to what we're doing, according to how old we are and according to our role in life. And I imagine, Socrates, the same goes for being *bad*.

72 a

SOCRATES: Well, what an amazing stroke of luck! There I was, looking for just one sort of 'being good,' and it turns out you've brought along a whole swarm of the things! ... But listen, Meno – my swarm analogy gives me an idea – suppose my question had been about bees, and exactly what it is to be a bee, and you'd started saying that there were 'lots of different kinds of bees'; what would you have said if I'd asked you this: 'Are you saying there are lots of different kinds of bees all differing from one another in their way of being bees? Or is the idea that, in that respect, there's no difference whatsoever from bee to bee, and that it's only in some other respect that they're different from one another, like, say, in how beautiful they are, or their size, or something else like that?' How would you have answered if you'd been asked that question?

b

MENO: That's just what I'd have said: no bee, in so far as it's a bee, is any different from any other bee.

SOCRATES: So, suppose that after that I said: 'In that case, Meno, just tell me about *that* – what's the respect in which there's no difference from bee to bee? What is it that makes all of them the same thing? What do you think that is?' Presumably you'd have been able to come up with something?

c

MENO: Yes.

SOCRATES: Well, do the same with cases of being good. Even if there are a lot of them, and lots of different sorts, they must at

least all have some single form,[5] something that makes them all cases of being good – and surely that's what it makes sense to focus on if you're explaining to someone what being good
d     actually is. Surely that's how you should answer the question. Or don't you understand what I'm saying?

MENO: I think so ... only, I don't see what you're asking me quite as fully as I'd like.

SOCRATES: Do you think this only applies to being good, Meno – that it's one thing for a man, and something else for a woman, and so on? Or do you think the same goes for being healthy, and being tall, and being strong? Do you think a man's health and a woman's health are two different things? Or is health the same form in every case – as long as it really
e     is health – whether it's in a man or in anyone else?

MENO: In the case of health, yes, I think it's the same thing for a man as for a woman.

SOCRATES: And will that be true for height and strength as well? If a woman is physically strong, will it be the same form – strength in exactly the same sense – that makes her strong? And what I mean when I say 'strength in exactly the same sense' is this: that strength doesn't have different ways of being strength, depending on whether it's in a man or a woman. Or do you think it does?

MENO: No, I don't.

73 a  SOCRATES: And what about being good? Whether it's in a child or an old man, a man or a woman, why should there be any difference in what makes it a case of being good?

MENO: Somehow I don't feel it works in quite the same way as those other things, Socrates.

SOCRATES: Oh? But weren't you saying that, for a man, being good means doing a good job of running a city, and for a woman it means doing a good job of running a household?

MENO: Yes.

SOCRATES: So is it possible to do a good job of running a city, or a home, or anything, if you don't do it sensibly and according to what's right?

MENO: Of course not.

b     SOCRATES: And if they do it sensibly and according to what's

right, then they'll be acting with good sense and with respect
for what's right?

MENO: Obviously.

SOCRATES: So that means both of them – men and women –
need the same things if they're going to be good people:
respect for what's right and good sense.

MENO: Apparently.

SOCRATES: What about children and old men? Surely there's
no way they could be good if they were out of control and
always doing wrong?

MENO: Of course not.

SOCRATES: No. They have to be sensible, and do what's right.

MENO: Yes.

SOCRATES: So it's the same for everyone, then: people are all    c
good in the same way, in the sense that it's by getting the
same qualities that they become good.

MENO: It looks like it.

SOCRATES: And obviously they wouldn't be 'good in the same
way' if it weren't the case that being good was the same thing
for all of them?

MENO: I suppose not.

SOCRATES: Well, in that case, since being good is the same
thing for everyone, try to remember Gorgias' definition – the
one you agree with.

MENO: Well, obviously being good is a matter of being able to
rule other people,[6] if what you're looking for is a single,    d
overall definition.

SOCRATES: That's exactly what I'm looking for. But wait – will
being a good child be the same, Meno? Or being a good
slave? – being able to rule* *your master*? Do you think you'd
still be a slave if you were the one doing the ruling?[7]

MENO: No, Socrates, obviously not.

SOCRATES: It does seem rather unlikely. And think about this,
too: 'being able to rule,' you say. Aren't we going to have to
add to that, '*according to what's right*, but *not if it means
doing wrong*'?

MENO: Yes, I suppose we are. After all, Socrates, doing what's
right is the same as being good, isn't it?[8]

e   SOCRATES: *The same as* being good, Meno? Or *one sort* of being good?[9]

MENO: How do you mean?

SOCRATES: Just what I'd mean with anything else. Take roundness, for example – I'd say that roundness was *one sort* of shape; I wouldn't simply say that roundness is *the same as shape*. And the reason I'd put it like that is because there are other shapes besides roundness.

MENO: Yes, good point . . . that's what I meant, as well; I'm saying there are other ways of being good besides doing what's right.

74 a   SOCRATES: What are they? Let's hear them. Just like the way I could name you some other shapes if you told me to – do the same for me, and tell me some other cases of being good.

MENO: All right, then: there's being brave. I think that's a form of being good; and being sensible, and having knowledge,[10] and being generous – and a whole lot of others.

SOCRATES: The same thing's happened to us again, Meno! We were looking for just *one* idea of being good, and we've found a whole load of them – though in a different sense from the way we did a moment ago. But we don't seem to be able to hit upon our single idea of being good that can cover all of them.

MENO: No, that's right, Socrates; I still can't do it the way you
b   want me to. I can't get just one, overall take on what it is to be good, the way I could with those other things.

SOCRATES: Well, never mind; that's only to be expected. I tell you what – I'll do my best and see if I can move us forward myself. You realize it's the same way with everything? Say someone asked you about the thing I mentioned a moment ago – 'What is *shape*, Meno?' – and you told him, 'roundness,' and then he'd said the same as I did: 'You mean, roundness is the same thing as shape, or one sort of shape?' You'd probably have said it was one sort of shape.

MENO: Absolutely.

c   SOCRATES: And that's because there are other shapes as well?

MENO: Yes.

SOCRATES: And if he'd gone on to ask what other shapes there are, you could have told him?

MENO: Yes, I could.

SOCRATES: And suppose he'd asked you in the same way about colour – 'What is colour?' – and you'd said, 'white,' and then he'd said, 'You mean, white is the same thing as colour, or just one sort of colour?' You'd have said it was one sort of colour, because there are other colours as well – right?

MENO: Right.

SOCRATES: And if he told you to name other colours, you could have named other colours – colours that are just as much    d colours as white is?

MENO: Yes.

SOCRATES: So suppose his approach to the question was the same as mine, and he said, 'Look, we keep arriving at *lots* of these things. That's not what I want. Try to do it like this: since you're referring to these lots of things by one and the same name, and saying that every one of them is a shape (even when they're completely different from one another), tell me what *that* is – the thing that includes both "round" and "straight", the thing you're calling "shape" when you say that "round is no more a shape than straight is." You do    e say that, don't you?'

MENO: Yes.

SOCRATES: So when you put it like that, are you saying that round is no more round than it is straight, and straight is no more straight than it is round?

MENO: Obviously not, Socrates.

SOCRATES: No. But what you are saying is that round is no more *a shape* than straight is, and vice versa?

MENO: That's right.

SOCRATES: 'Well, what's that – the thing that "shape" is the name for? Try and tell me.' Now if that's what he was asking,    75 a either about shape or about colour, and you said, 'I'm sorry, but I don't understand what you want. I don't know what you mean!', he'd probably have been amazed. 'You don't understand? You don't understand that I'm just trying to find out what it is that all of them have in common?' Or even with these examples, Meno, would you have no idea what to say? – if someone asked, 'What is it in round, and straight, and all the other things you call "shapes", that's the same in all of them?' Go on, try and tell me. That way you'll also get a bit of practice for your answer about being good.

b  MENO: I've got a better idea. Why don't you tell *me*, Socrates?

SOCRATES: You want me to pamper you, do you?

MENO: Of course.

SOCRATES: And then you'll tell me what being good is? Will you?

MENO: I will, I promise.

SOCRATES: Well, I better give it a try, then – that's quite a bargain.

MENO: It certainly is.

SOCRATES: All right, let's see then; let me try and tell you what shape is. See if you accept this as a definition: let's say that shape is . . . the only thing that colour always comes with.[11] There. Is that good enough for you, or are you looking for

c  something different? I'd be very happy if you gave me a definition of being good along those lines.

MENO: But that's a *silly* definition, Socrates!

SOCRATES: What do you mean?

MENO: Well, a shape – according to your idea – is 'the thing colour always comes with'. Fine. But what if someone says they don't know what colour is? What if they're as baffled about that as they are about shape? What kind of an answer do you think you'd give them?

SOCRATES: Well, one that's true, at least. And if the man who'd asked the question was one of those expert quibblers,[12] who just want to 'win' arguments, then what I'd say to him is this:

d  'Look, I've made my claim. If what I'm saying isn't right, that's your problem: it's up to you to question me and prove me wrong.' But if the two of us were friends and wanted to talk things through with one another – the way you and I are doing now – then I'd have to go a bit easier on him and answer in a more *talk-it-through* kind of way.[13] And I suppose 'a more talk-it-through kind of way' means not just giving an answer that's true but also only answering by way of things the other person admits he knows, when you ask him. *

So I'll try to tell you what a shape is that way. Tell me – do
you know what an edge is? I mean, in the sense of a border,    e
or an outline? I'm treating all those as meaning the same
thing – Prodicus[14] might disagree with us; but I assume you
talk about things having a border or coming to an edge?
That's the kind of thing I mean. Nothing fancy.

MENO: Yes, I do. I think I understand what you mean.

SOCRATES: And you talk about surfaces, and also solids? As    76 a
in, those things you find in geometry?

MENO: Yes.

SOCRATES: Well, you're already there, then: you can use those
to understand what I mean by shape. Because here's what
I'm saying holds true for every shape: I'm saying that a shape
is the thing that borders a solid. So I could say, in short, that
a shape is a border of a solid.

MENO: And what's your definition of colour, Socrates?

SOCRATES: Show a little respect, Meno! Look at you, pestering
a poor old man with all these questions; meanwhile you
refuse to remember, and tell me, what Gorgias says being    b
good is!

MENO: But I will, Socrates – just as soon as you've told me
what colour is.

SOCRATES: Even with a blindfold on, Meno, anyone could tell
just from talking to you that you're beautiful, and men still
fall for you.

MENO: Why's that?

SOCRATES: Because you're always so bossy in conversation!
And that's what people do when they're spoiled – spoiled
from being treated like royalty while they're young and sexy.
Plus you've probably noticed I can't resist beautiful people.    c
All right, I'll pamper you and answer the question.

MENO: Yes, good idea. Pamper me.

SOCRATES: So do you want me to answer the way Gorgias
would? That'll make it easiest for you to follow.

MENO: Well, of course.

SOCRATES: All right. So do you two talk about 'out-flowings'
from things, the way Empedocles does?[15]

MENO: Now you're talking!

SOCRATES: And 'channels', into which, and out through which, the 'out-flowings' pass?

MENO: Absolutely.

SOCRATES: And of these out-flowings, some of them fit some
d    of the channels, while some are too big or too small?

MENO: That's right.

SOCRATES: And you know what I mean by 'sight'?

MENO: Yes.

SOCRATES: Well, from all of that you can 'throw together what I mean', as Pindar says. Because here's what colour is: *a sight-fitting, perceptible out-flowing from shapes*.

MENO: I think that's a fantastic answer, Socrates!

SOCRATES: Maybe that's because it's in the sort of language you're more used to; plus, I suspect you realize you could
e    also use it to say what sound is, and smell, and lots of other things like that.

MENO: Absolutely.

SOCRATES: It's a theatrical answer,[16] Meno. That's why you like it more than the one about shape.

MENO: I do.

SOCRATES: But what it isn't, son of Alexidemus, is a better answer. I'm convinced the other one was better. And I believe you'd come to think so too, if you didn't have to leave town (as you were telling me yesterday) before the *Mysteries*[17] – if only you could stay and be initiated.

77 a  MENO: I would stay, Socrates, if you told me lots more things like that last one!

SOCRATES: Well, I'll certainly try to. I'll do my very best, for your sake and my own. But I may not be able to come up with many more ideas like that one. Anyway, come on, it's your turn now: you've got to try to keep your promise and tell me what being good is, as a whole. Stop 'making lots of things from one', as the jokers say to someone who's smashed a plate. Just leave it whole, and in one piece, and tell me what
b    it is. You've got your examples from me now.

MENO: All right, Socrates. I think that being good, as that poet says, is a matter of

Rejoicing in all that is fair and fine, and being able.[18]

That's what I say 'being good' is, as well – wanting fine things and being able to acquire them.

SOCRATES: By 'someone who wants *fine* things' you mean someone who wants things that are good?

MENO: Yes, exactly.

SOCRATES: You mean, as if some people want bad things, and only some of us want good things? Don't you think that everyone wants what's good?

MENO: No, I don't think so.

SOCRATES: What – people sometimes want things that are bad?

MENO: Yes.

SOCRATES: Because they reckon the bad things are good, you mean? Or do they realize they're bad and want them anyway?

MENO: [*Thinks it over for a moment.*] Both, I think.

SOCRATES: What? You really think, Meno, that a person can realize bad things are bad and want them anyway?

MENO: Definitely.

SOCRATES: When you say someone can 'want' bad things, you mean, want to get them?

MENO: Yes, to get them. What else?

SOCRATES: Why? Because they reckon these bad things *benefit* whoever gets them? Or do they realize that bad things always harm whoever's got them?

MENO: Well, in some of these cases, people think the bad things are doing them good, but in other cases, they know they're doing them harm.

SOCRATES: And, in your view, do the people who think bad things are doing them good realize the bad things are bad?

MENO: No, I certainly wouldn't say that.

SOCRATES: Well, clearly those people don't *want* bad things (the people who don't realize that they're bad). They want things that they thought were good – it's just that those things are, in fact, bad. That's to say, if they don't realize these things are bad, and think they're good, then it's clear that what they actually want is what's good. Don't you see?

MENO: Yes, that's probably right – in their case.

SOCRATES: And what about the ones who do want bad things
– you say – and at the same time believe that bad things harm
whoever gets them? Presumably they're aware that they're
going to be harmed by the things they want?

78 a    MENO: Yes, they must be.

SOCRATES: And don't these people think that being harmed
makes you, to the extent that you're harmed, a loser?[19]

MENO: Yes, they must think that, as well.

SOCRATES: And don't they think that losers are sad and
pathetic?

MENO: Yes, I suppose so.

SOCRATES: So does anyone actually *want to be* a sad, pathetic
loser?

MENO: No, I suppose not, Socrates.

SOCRATES: Well, nobody wants bad things, then, if we're sure
that nobody wants to be someone like that. I mean, isn't that
just what being a loser is – wanting bad things and then
getting them?[20]

b    MENO: You're probably right, Socrates; I guess no one wants
bad things.

SOCRATES: Right. So were you saying just a moment ago that
being good means 'wanting good things, and being able . . .'?

MENO: Yes, that's what I said.

SOCRATES: So out of that definition, the 'wanting' part already
applies to everyone from the start[21] – so in that respect no
one's a better person than anyone else?

MENO: Apparently not.

SOCRATES: So if anyone's a better person than someone else,
it's obviously because of the 'being able' part?

MENO: Exactly.

SOCRATES: So that means that the quality of being good, on

c    your definition, is just *the ability to acquire good things*?

MENO: Yes! I like the way you're thinking, Socrates: that's my
view exactly![22]

SOCRATES: All right then, let's look at what you're saying and
see if you're right. You may very well be on to something.
You're saying that being good means being able to acquire
good things?

MENO: That's right.

SOCRATES: And by 'good things' you mean things like health and money? Right?

MENO: Yes – gold and silver; that's what I'm talking about; and obtaining positions of power and honour in your city.[23]

SOCRATES: I see. So there's nothing else you're thinking of as good, besides those kinds of things?

MENO: No. All the things I'm talking about are like that.          d

SOCRATES: Right. So being a good man means acquiring loads of gold and silver, according to Meno, special family friend of the Great King![24] And are you including with this idea of 'acquiring things', Meno, that you have to do it according to what's right, and with respect for religion? Or doesn't that matter? Are you just as happy to call it 'being good' even if you acquire things *wrongfully*?

MENO: No, of course not, Socrates.

SOCRATES: You'd call that *being bad*?

MENO: Well, obviously.

SOCRATES: So it looks like this 'acquiring' business also has to involve respect for what's right, or moderation, or religiousness, or some other part of being a good person.  e Otherwise, it won't count as being good, even if it *does* supply you with lots of good things.

MENO: Of course. How could it possibly count as being good without those?

SOCRATES: And what about *not acquiring* any gold or silver, either for yourself or for someone else, when it isn't right to do so? Won't that count as being good – that particular case of *not acquiring anything*?

MENO: Yes, it seems so.

SOCRATES: So in other words, being good isn't a matter of acquiring those sorts of good things any more than *not* acquiring them. It looks like acquiring things will only count as being good when it's done with respect for what's right; but when it's done without anything like that, it'll be a case of being *bad*.                                                      79 a

MENO: Yes, I suppose that must be right.

SOCRATES: So, weren't we saying just a little while ago that each of those things – respect for what's right, and moderation, and so on – is part of being a good person?

MENO: Yes.

SOCRATES: I see, Meno – you're playing games with me, are you?

MENO: Why do you say that, Socrates?

SOCRATES: Well, look; just a moment ago I asked you not to split up the idea of being good – not to break it into little pieces; I even gave you examples of how you were supposed to answer. And without paying any attention to that, you're now telling me that being good means 'being able to acquire
b   good things *with respect for what's right*' – which you say is part of being good.

MENO: Yes, that's right.

SOCRATES: So it turns out, from all the things that you're agreeing to, that being good just means doing – with some 'part of being good' – whatever it is you're doing. Because that's what you're calling respect for what's right (and each of those qualities): 'part of being good'.

MENO: So what's your point?*

SOCRATES: My point is, I asked you to tell me what being good is, as a whole; and without even coming close to telling me what it is itself, you're now saying that any action counts as being good as long as it's done with one of the parts of being
c   good – as if you'd already told me what being good is as a whole and I'm going to have any idea what you're talking about when you go and chop it up into parts! So it looks to me like you'll have to go back and answer the same question, Meno. What *is* being good – granted that 'any action that's done with a part of being good counts as being good'? Because that's all we're saying when we say that 'doing anything with respect for what's right counts as being good.' Or am I wrong? Don't you think we need to ask the same question? Do you think anyone's going to know what a *part* of being good is if they don't know what being good is, itself?[25]

MENO: No, I suppose not.

d   SOCRATES: No. And in fact, if you remember, when I gave you

that answer about shape, a little while back,[26] we rejected
that way of answering – I mean, where you try to answer a
question by using things that are still being figured out and
haven't yet been agreed on.

MENO: And we were right to reject that way of answering,
Socrates.

SOCRATES: Well, stop doing it yourself, then! If we're still
trying to find out what *being good* is, as a whole, don't go
thinking that you'll be showing anyone what it is if you talk
about *parts* of it in your answer (or that you'll ever explain
anything if you make your claims that way). We'll just need    e
to go back and ask the same question: you're talking about
'parts of being good', but what's that? What *is* being good?
Or do you think I'm talking nonsense?

MENO: No. I suppose you're right.

SOCRATES: In that case, you'd better answer the question again,
from the top: What do you think being good is – you and
your mate Gorgias?

MENO: You know, people kept telling me, Socrates, even before
I met you, that all you do is go around being baffled by things    80 a
and baffling everyone else. And now that I've met you, sure
enough, I feel as though you're bewitching me, and jinxing
me, and casting some strange spell over me, to the point
where I'm about as baffled as can be. You know what I think?
Just to tease you a little – I think that you're exactly like that
flat-faced numbfish.[27] You certainly look like a numbfish,
and you're just the same in other ways as well: because you
know what a numbfish does? It makes anyone that gets too
close and touches it, go numb; and that's pretty much what
I think you've done to me. My mind and my tongue have
literally gone numb. I've got no idea how to answer the    b
question. And yet, damn it, I've talked about 'being a good
man' *thousands* of times. I've made countless claims about
it, time and again, in front of loads of people, and perfectly
good claims, too – or so I thought at the time. But now I
can't even say what it is. I haven't got the faintest idea! If
you ask me, you're making a smart decision in not going on

any trips away from Athens, or living abroad; because if you did this sort of thing in some other city, as a foreigner, you'd probably be locked up for being a wizard.

SOCRATES: Oh, that's very crafty, Meno. I almost fell for it.

MENO: Fell for what, Socrates?

c   SOCRATES: I know exactly why you compared me to a numbfish.

MENO: Why?

SOCRATES: To get me to compare you to something in return. That's one thing I've learned about all beautiful people: oh, they just love it when you tell them what they look like. It's all right for them; because of course beautiful people are always told they resemble beautiful things. Well, sorry: I'm not going to compare you to anything. And as for me – unless a numbfish feels numb itself when it makes other people feel numb, then I'm not like a numbfish. Because it's not as if I've got all the answers myself when I baffle other people. I only make other people feel baffled by being more baffled than anyone myself. Take our question about what exactly being

d   good is: I certainly don't know the answer, and that's why you . . . well, maybe you knew before you 'touched' me, but right now you're very like a man who doesn't know. Of course, I'm still willing to look into it with you; I still want the two of us to try to find out what it is.

MENO: But how can you try to find out about something, Socrates, if you 'haven't got the faintest idea' what it is? I mean, how can you put before your mind a thing *that you have no knowledge of*, in order to try to find out about it? And even supposing you did come across it, how would you know that *that* was *it*, if you didn't know what it was to begin with?

e   SOCRATES: Ah, I see what you're getting at, Meno. See what you're doing? You're bringing in that famous quibbler's argu-ment, the one that says that it's impossible to try to find out about anything – either what you know or what you don't know. 'You can't try to find out about something you know about, because you know about it, in which case there's no point trying to find out about it; and you can't try to find out

about something you don't know about, either, because then
you don't even know what it is you're trying to find out
about.'[28]

MENO: And you don't think that's a good argument, Socrates?    81 a

SOCRATES: Nope.

MENO: Can you tell me why not?

SOCRATES: Yes, I can. It's because I've listened to certain men
and women, people who know all about the world of the
gods . . .

MENO: Saying what? What claim did they make?

SOCRATES: A claim, in my view, that was as beautiful as it was
true.

MENO: What claim? What people?

SOCRATES: Well, the people who make the claim are all those
priests and priestesses who've taken the trouble to be able to
explain the basis of their religious practices. And Pindar[29]
says the same thing, and so do lots of other poets – all the    b
ones inspired by the gods. And what they say is this (you
decide if you think that what they say is true): they say that
a person's soul can never die; that sometimes it comes to an
end – most people call it 'dying' – and sometimes it comes
back into being, but that it's never destroyed. And that's why
we've got to live the whole of our lives as religiously as we
possibly can. Because only those

> who've paid Persephone the price,
> for the pain, for the grief, of long ago[30] –
> theirs are the souls that she sends,
> when the ninth year comes,
> back to the sun-lit world above.
> And from those souls, proud-hearted kings will rise,    c
> and the swift and strong, and the wisest of the wise.
> And people, for the rest of time,
> will hail them as heroes, to be held in awe.

So, since the soul can never die, and has been born over
and over again, and has already seen what there is in this
world, and what there is in the world beyond – i.e. absolutely

everything – there's nothing it hasn't already learned about.
So it wouldn't be at all surprising if it managed to remember
things, the things it used to know, either about being good
or about anything else. Because if the whole of nature is akin,
d      and your soul has already learned and understood everything,
there's no reason why you shouldn't be able, after remembering just *one* thing – most people call it 'learning' – to go
on and figure out everything else, as long as you're adventur-
ous and don't get tired of trying to find out about things; in
fact, 'finding out about things' and 'learning' are entirely a
matter of remembering. So you shouldn't pay attention to
that quibbler's argument. That claim is just an excuse for
being lazy, and music to the ears of slackers; whereas mine
gives us reason to be energetic and eager to find out as much
e      as we can. And it's the one I trust and believe is true, and
that's why I'm willing to try and find out what being good is
– with your help.

MENO: Yes, all right, Socrates ... but what do you mean by
this idea that we don't *learn* anything, and that what we call
learning is just remembering? I'd like to learn a bit more
about that. Is that really how it is?

SOCRATES: Didn't I just say you were crafty, Meno? There you
82 a    go again – asking me if you can '*learn* more', when I've just said
there's no such thing as learning, only remembering! You're
trying to trick me into contradicting myself straight away!

MENO: No, Socrates, that wasn't what I was thinking, I swear!
I just used that expression out of habit. All I meant was, if
you've got some way of *showing* me that what you say is
true, then I'd like to hear it.

SOCRATES: Well, it's certainly not easy. But all right, I'm willing
to give it a try, just for you ... [*He looks over at the large
b      group of slaves that Meno has with him*] – Do me a favour
and call over one of these attendants of yours, whichever one
you like. I'll use him for a demonstration.

MENO: No problem. [*He beckons to one of his slaves.*] Come
over here!

[*The slave joins them.*]

SOCRATES: Is he Greek, at least? Does he speak Greek?

MENO: Absolutely. He's a home-bred.[31]

SOCRATES: All right. Now watch carefully, and see if he gives the impression of remembering things or learning them from me.

MENO: I will.

SOCRATES: Tell me then, boy[32] – do you know what a square is? You know that a square . . . [*He draws a square in the sand with his stick.*] . . . looks like this?

SLAVE: Yes.

SOCRATES: So a square is a figure with four sides – these lines  c here – all the same length?

SLAVE: Of course.

SOCRATES: And these lines that go through the middle [*fg and tu*] – they're the same length as well, aren't they?

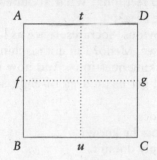

SLAVE: Yes.

SOCRATES: Right. Now a figure like this could be various different sizes, couldn't it?

SLAVE: Of course.

SOCRATES: So suppose this side here [*BC*] was two feet long, and that side there [*AB*] was two feet long, how many square feet would the whole thing be? [*The slave looks unsure.*] Here, look at it like this: suppose it was two feet long on this side [*BC*] but only one foot long on this side [*fB*], wouldn't that make the area one-times-two square feet?

SLAVE: Yes.                                                                                          d

SOCRATES: But since it's two feet long on this side as well [*AB*], doesn't that make it *two*-times-two?

SLAVE: Yes.

SOCRATES: So that gives us two-times-two square feet?

SLAVE: Yes.

SOCRATES: So how much is two-times-two? Figure it out, and tell me.

SLAVE: Four, Socrates.

SOCRATES: All right. Now can you imagine there being another square, also with four equal sides, just like this one, but twice the area?

SLAVE: Yes.

SOCRATES: So how many square feet would that one be?

SLAVE: Eight square feet.

SOCRATES: All right, now listen: try and tell me how long each
e       *side* of that one would have to be. Look – each side of this one here is two feet long. What about each side of a square that's twice the area?

SLAVE: That's obvious, Socrates: twice as long.

SOCRATES: You see, Meno? I'm not teaching him anything. All I'm doing is asking questions. And now he thinks he knows which line will get us an area of eight square feet. Doesn't he?

MENO: Yes, he does.

SOCRATES: So does he know?

MENO: He certainly doesn't.

SOCRATES: But he *thinks* he knows we'll need a line that's twice as long?

MENO: Yes.

SOCRATES: Just watch him then, as he remembers, step by step – the way remembering should be done. [*He turns back to the slave.*] Now, you, tell me: you're saying that from a line
83 a     that's twice the length we'll get twice the area? Here's what I mean: it can't be longer on one side and shorter on the other; it's got to be the same length on all four sides, just like this one here [ABCD] but twice the area – *eight square feet.* Now take your time: you still think it'll be from a line that's twice as long as this one?

SLAVE: Yes.

SOCRATES: All right. And don't we get a line twice as long as this one if we just add on another line of the same length, here [CW]?

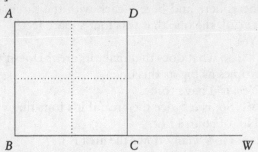

SLAVE: Yes, of course.

SOCRATES: So you're saying that from this line here [BW] we'll get our area of eight square feet – i.e. if we have four of these lines, all the same length as this one [BW]?

SLAVE: Yes.

SOCRATES: Let's mark up four equal lines, then, starting off from this one [BW] . . . [*He begins to draw the larger square, BWXY.*] . . . So that would make this square here [BWXY] the one you're saying has an area of eight square feet – yes?

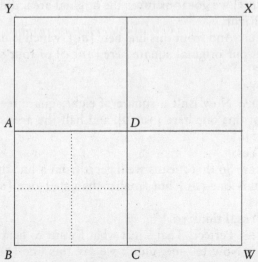

SLAVE: Absolutely.

SOCRATES: All right. Now isn't it made up of four squares – here, here, here and here – each with the same area as this one [ABCD], the one that was four square feet?

SLAVE: Yes.

SOCRATES: So what does that make its area? Doesn't that make it four times as big as this one?

SLAVE: Yes, it'd have to be.

SOCRATES: So, is it twice the area, if it's four times as big?

SLAVE: No, of course not.

SOCRATES: How many times the area is it?

SLAVE: Four times the area.

c    SOCRATES: Ah. So it turns out we don't get twice the area from a line twice as long. We get four times the area. Right, boy?

SLAVE: Yes, that's right.

SOCRATES: Because four times four is sixteen square feet. Isn't it?

SLAVE: Yes.

SOCRATES: In that case, which line will give us our square of eight square feet? [*The slave looks unsure.*] From this line here [BW] we got four times the original area, didn't we?

SLAVE: Right.

SOCRATES: And from this line here [BC], which is half as long, we get our original square here [ABCD] of four square feet. Right?

SLAVE: Yes.

SOCRATES: Now isn't a square of eight square feet twice the area of this one here [ABCD], and half the area of that one [BWXY]?

SLAVE: Yes.

SOCRATES: So that means we'll get it from a line that's bigger than this one [BC] but smaller than that one [BW]. Won't we?

d    SLAVE: Yes, I think so.

SOCRATES: Perfect! That's just what I want to hear: what *you* think.[33] Now tell me; didn't we say this line [BC] was two feet long, and that one [BW] was four feet long?

SLAVE: Yes.

SOCRATES: So that means the line we're trying to find has got to be bigger than this line here – i.e. more than two feet long – and smaller than that one – i.e. less than four feet long?

SLAVE: Yes, it does.

SOCRATES: So, try and tell me how long you think it is.                    e

SLAVE: [*Tentatively*] *Three* feet long?

SOCRATES: All right. So let's say it's three feet long ... why don't we just take half of this line here and add it on, and that'll make three feet. [*He means, add half of* CW – *i.e.* CK – *to* BC]. Look: two feet here [BC] plus one foot here [CK]. And we'll do the same on this side – two feet here [AB] plus one [AM]. [*He now draws the square* KLMB]. That gives us the square you mean.

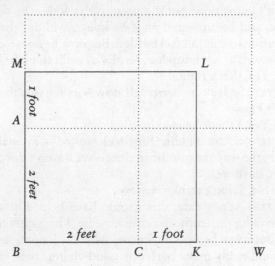

SLAVE: Yes.

SOCRATES: Right. Now, if it's three feet long on this side, and three feet long on this side, doesn't that give the whole thing an area of three-times-three square feet?

SLAVE: It looks like it.

SOCRATES: And how much is three-times-three square feet?

SLAVE: Nine.

SOCRATES: And how many square feet was our twice-as-big square supposed to be?

SLAVE: Eight.

SOCRATES: Ah. So we still haven't got our square of eight square feet; we don't get it from the three-foot line either.

SLAVE: No, we don't.

SOCRATES: Well, what line do we get it from? Try and tell us
84 a    exactly. And if you don't want to use numbers, you can just show us. [*He hands the slave his stick.*] What line?

SLAVE: [*He stares at the drawing.*] Honest to god, Socrates, I don't know!

SOCRATES: There, see that, Meno? You realize where he is now on the road towards remembering? At first, he didn't know which line gave us an area of eight square feet ... and he still doesn't know now; but the point is, back then he *thought* he knew, and he answered as if he knew, without the slightest hesitation – he didn't feel baffled. But now he *does* feel baffled;
b       and as well as not knowing, he also doesn't think he knows.

MENO: Yes, that's right.

SOCRATES: So isn't he better off now – as regards the thing he didn't know?

MENO: Yes, I think he is.

SOCRATES: So by making him feel baffled – by making him numb, the way the numbfish does – we haven't done him any harm, have we?

MENO: No, I don't think we have.

SOCRATES: At any rate, this should have helped him towards discovering the truth. Because now he'll be happy to try and find out what he doesn't know, whereas before, he thought
c       he could easily make perfectly good claims, time and again, in front of loads of people, all about how you need a line of twice the length to get twice the area.[34]

MENO: Yes, probably!

SOCRATES: So do you think he would ever have tried to find out, or learn, what he wrongly thought he knew, before he tumbled into bafflement – before he sensed he didn't know and felt the need to know?

MENO: No, I don't think he would, Socrates.

SOCRATES: So in fact, being numbed was good for him?

MENO: I think it was.

SOCRATES: Then look at what comes next: out of being baffled, see what he'll also discover by searching with my help – and all I'll be doing is asking questions; I won't be teaching him. Watch very closely. See if you catch me teaching him or explaining things at any stage, and not simply bringing out his own opinions. [*He turns back to the slave.*] You: tell me ... [*He draws a new square, the same size as the first one.*] ... we've got our square of four square feet, here. Right? Understand?

SLAVE: I understand.

SOCRATES: And we could add another one next to it, here, the same size?

SLAVE: Yes.

SOCRATES: And a third one, here, the same size as each of these two? [*The drawing now looks like this:*]

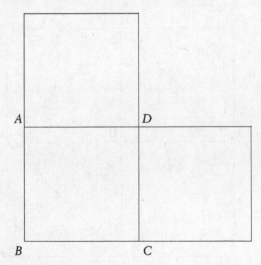

SLAVE: Yes.

SOCRATES: All right. And we could fill in the other one here in the corner?

SLAVE: Of course.

SOCRATES: So wouldn't that give us four squares, all with the same area?

e SLAVE: Yes.

SOCRATES: So how many times the area of this one [ABCD] does that make the whole thing?

SLAVE: Four times the area.

SOCRATES: And what we needed was a square that was *twice* the area. Remember?

SLAVE: Absolutely.

SOCRATES: All right. Now can we also have a line like this, cutting each one of these squares in two, from corner to

85 a corner?* [*He draws the line AC, then the three other similar lines, CG, GT and TA.*]

SLAVE: Yes.

SOCRATES: Right, so that gives us these four equal lines, with this new square, here, inside them? [*He means the lines AC, CG, GT and TA, enclosing the square ACGT.*]

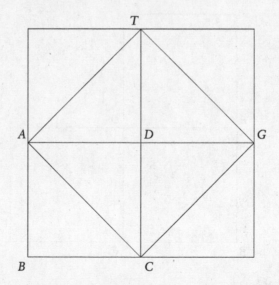

SLAVE: Yes, it does.

SOCRATES: Now think what's that square's area [ACGT]?

SLAVE: [*Hesitates*] I don't follow.

SOCRATES: Look, isn't one half of each of these four smaller
   squares now on the inside, sliced off by each one of these
   lines?

SLAVE: Yes.

SOCRATES: So how many of those chunks [*i.e. of the triangles*]
   are in this square here [*ACGT*]?

SLAVE: Four.

SOCRATES: And how many are there in this one here [*ABCD*]?

SLAVE: Two.

SOCRATES: And four is how many times bigger than two?

SLAVE: Twice as big.

SOCRATES: So what's this square's area [*ACGT*]?

SLAVE: [*Thinks for a moment*]: Eight square feet!                     b

SOCRATES: And what line do we get it from?

SLAVE: That one there [*AC*]!

SOCRATES: The one that stretches from corner to corner in the
   square of four square feet?

SLAVE: Yes.

SOCRATES: They call that line a 'diagonal' – sophists, I mean.
   So if we're calling that line a 'diagonal', then it's from the
   diagonal of a square, *according to you*, Meno's boy, that we
   get a square that's twice the area?

SLAVE: Yes, Socrates. Absolutely.

SOCRATES: What do you think, Meno? Did he say anything in
   his answers that wasn't his own opinion?

MENO: No; they were all his own opinions.[35]                          c

SOCRATES: And we're quite sure he didn't have knowledge –
   we were saying so a moment ago.

MENO: That's right.

SOCRATES: But these opinions were certainly there, inside him?
   Weren't they?

MENO: Yes.

SOCRATES: So in other words, inside someone with no knowledge (of whatever it might be) there are correct opinions
   about the things he doesn't know?

MENO: So it seems.

SOCRATES: And although right now he'll find these opinions

are hazy and dreamlike (because they've only just been stirred up), if you ask him the same questions over and over again, and in lots of different ways, you can be sure that he'd end
d     up knowing about these things as precisely as anyone.

MENO: Yes, he probably would.

SOCRATES: So that means he'll have knowledge without anyone having taught him, just through being asked questions – by retrieving the knowledge from within himself?

MENO: Yes.

SOCRATES: And isn't retrieving knowledge from inside yourself the same thing as remembering?

MENO: Absolutely.

SOCRATES: So this knowledge that he has within him – presumably he either acquired it at some point, or he's had it forever?[36]

MENO: That's right.

SOCRATES: So if he's had it forever, then he's also been, forever, a being with knowledge; and if he acquired it at some point, it certainly can't have been during the life he's living now.[37]
e     Or has someone taught him geometry? Because he'll do exactly the same thing with any question in geometry, and with every single other subject as well. So is there someone who's taught him – taught him everything? You should know, especially if he was born and raised in your own home.

MENO: I know for a fact that no one's ever taught him.

SOCRATES: But he does have these opinions, doesn't he?

MENO: It seems he must, Socrates.

SOCRATES: And if he didn't acquire them in his present life,
86 a   doesn't that prove that he had them – had already learned them – in some other period of time?

MENO: Apparently.

SOCRATES: And that other time must be the time when he wasn't human?

MENO: Yes.

SOCRATES: So if he's had these correct opinions somewhere inside him, for all the time that he's been a human being and for all the time that he hasn't – opinions that become bits of knowledge when they're roused by questioning – won't that mean there's never been a time when his soul hadn't already learned them? Because, obviously, it's for the whole of time that he either has or hasn't been in human form.

MENO: Yes, that seems to follow.

SOCRATES: So if the truth about how things really are has been b in our soul forever, then the soul must be ever-living – and that means that if there's something you happen not to know right now, or rather, happen not to have remembered yet, you mustn't be afraid to try and find out about it – that is, to remember it.

MENO: Socrates ... in a funny kind of way ... I like what you're saying.

SOCRATES: I like what I'm saying, too, Meno. And I wouldn't absolutely insist on all the other details if I was defending my claim; but the idea that we'd be better people – more energetic, less lazy – if we felt that it was our duty to try to find out whatever we don't know, instead of thinking that discovering what we don't know isn't even possible, and that c there's no point in even trying – that's a claim I will keep fighting for, as best I can, in everything I say and do.

MENO: And I certainly think you're right about that, too, Socrates.

SOCRATES: Well, since we're agreeing that you've always got to try and find out what you don't know, why don't the two of us have another go at trying to find out what being good is?

MENO: Sure ... although, mind you, Socrates, what I'd really like to look into, and hear more about, is the question I asked back at the start – whether what we're dealing with is something that can be taught, or if being good just comes to d people naturally ... or how exactly?

SOCRATES: If only I could control *you*, Meno, instead of only controlling myself! If I could, we wouldn't look into whether being good is or isn't teachable until we'd first tried to find out what it is. As it is, although you don't even try to control yourself – because you prefer to be 'free'[38] – you certainly try to control *me,* and you're very good at it. So I'll grant you

e

your wish. Do I have any choice? So it seems we have to consider what sort of thing it is, even though we don't yet know *what* it is. But at least relax your power over me just a little and grant me this: let's ask the question – the question of whether it's teachable – *on a hypothesis*.[39] And when I say 'on a hypothesis', I mean the way mathematicians often look at problems, when someone asks them a question ... about an area, for example ... like 'Can this area here be inscribed,

87 a

as a triangle, in this circle?' A mathematician might say, 'Well, I don't know yet; maybe it can, maybe it can't, but I think I have a *hypothesis* that will help with the problem, and it goes like this:

> IF *the area is such that, when you stretch it out along its given line, it falls short by an area matching the area stretched along the line, then I take that to give us one outcome ... and we get another outcome, if that can't be done to it.*[40]

So, on that hypothesis, I'm prepared to tell you the outcome

b

– whether or not it's possible for the area to be inscribed in the circle.' We can do the same thing with our question about being good: since we don't know what it is, or what sort of thing it is, let's first find a hypothesis and then use that to look at whether or not it's teachable. Here's what we say:

> *Being good (which is a feature of the soul) will turn out to be teachable, or unteachable, IF – what? What sort of feature of the soul would it have to be?*

Here's a place to start, then: will it or won't it be teachable

c

... (or *remember-able*, as we were saying just now; but let's say it doesn't matter which word we use) ... will it be teachable if it's something different from knowledge? Presumably not. Isn't it obvious to anyone that the only thing you can be taught is knowledge?

MENO: Yes, that's right.

SOCRATES: But if being good *is* a kind of knowledge, obviously that would mean it *is* teachable?

MENO: Of course.

SOCRATES: So, that's quickly dealt with, then. We're sure that

*IF it's a kind of knowledge, **then** it can be taught; and if it isn't, then it can't?*

MENO: Absolutely.

SOCRATES: So it looks like the next thing we need to think about is whether being good is a kind of knowledge or something different from knowledge. Right?

MENO: Right. There's our next question.                          d

SOCRATES: Well, how about this – are we saying that being a good person is something that's good? Can we treat that as a stable 'hypothesis': that it's a good thing?[41]

MENO: Absolutely.

SOCRATES: Right; so if there's anything that's good in life that has nothing whatsoever to do with knowledge, then being good could well turn out not to be any kind of knowledge. But if there's *nothing* good in life that isn't in the general sphere of knowledge,[42] then a hunch that it's some kind of knowledge would be a pretty good hunch?

MENO: Yes, that's right.

SOCRATES: Now obviously, being good is what makes us good people.

MENO: Yes.

SOCRATES: And if we are good, we do good.[43] Because all good   e
things do us good, don't they?[44]

MENO: Yes.

SOCRATES: Which means that being good people must also do us good.

MENO: It must . . . from what we've agreed.

SOCRATES: Then here's our next question: What kinds of things do us good in life? Let's run through them, one by one. There's being healthy, being strong, being beautiful and – of course – being rich. We say that things like that do us good in life, don't we?

MENO: Yes, we do.                                                88 a

SOCRATES: But we also say that the very same things sometimes do us harm – or don't you think so?

MENO: No, I agree.

SOCRATES: Well, ask yourself this, then: When do they do us good, and when do they do us harm? In each case, what has to be guiding us? Don't those things only do us any good when we're guided by a sense of the right way to use them – otherwise they do us harm?

MENO: Yes, exactly.

SOCRATES: All right then, now let's look at features of the soul.[45] You're familiar with things like self-control, respect for what's right, bravery, academic ability, a good memory, generosity – all those sorts of things?

b  MENO: Yes.

SOCRATES: Now think about the ones you take to be something other than knowledge – can't they sometimes do us harm as well as doing us good? Take bravery, for example, if we treat bravery as being a sort of fearlessness rather than a kind of wisdom:[46] isn't it the case that when you're fearless without any sense, you get hurt, and when you're fearless with sense, it does you good?

MENO: Yes.

SOCRATES: And isn't it the same with self-control or academic ability? Surely learning things, or training yourself, only does you any good when it has some sense to it? If there's no sense in it, then it does you harm?

MENO: Yes, that's absolutely right.

c  SOCRATES: So, in general, all the strivings and perseverings of our soul only result in our having a good life[47] if wisdom is showing us the way; but when foolishness is guiding us, they have the opposite effect.

MENO: It looks that way.

SOCRATES: So if being good is one of the features of the soul, and one that necessarily does us good, then it must be a form of wisdom – seeing as all these other aspects of the soul don't, in and of themselves,[48] do us either any good or harm; they're

d      only able to do us any good or do us harm when they're combined with wisdom or foolishness. So by that argument, if being good is definitely something that does us good, it's got to be some form of wisdom?

MENO: Yes, I think that's right.

SOCRATES: And what about all those other things – being rich and so on – that we said just now are sometimes good for us and sometimes harmful? Shall we say that, just as wisdom guides the rest of the soul and makes sure all aspects of the soul are doing us good (while foolishness makes them harmful), in the same way, the soul also has to use those external things in the right way and guide us in our use of them, if they're to do us any good; but without the right sort of guidance from the soul, they do us harm?

MENO: Absolutely.

SOCRATES: And it's a soul with wisdom that gives the right sort of guidance, and an unwise soul that makes mistakes, and guides us badly?

MENO: That's right.

SOCRATES: So that means we can make this overall claim: that the value of everything else in life hangs on the soul, and the value of every aspect of the soul itself hangs on wisdom. So by that argument, it seems that wisdom is *the* thing that does us good in life. And being good people, we say, does us good?

MENO: Absolutely.

SOCRATES: So in other words, we must think that being good is a kind of wisdom, either entirely or partly?[49]

MENO: Yes, Socrates; what we're saying sounds pretty good to me.

SOCRATES: So if that's the case, it can't be that good people are naturally good.[50]

MENO: No, they can't be.

SOCRATES: In any case, there's another problem with that: if the good did become good naturally, surely there'd be people whose job was to spot the children who were born to be good, and once they'd picked them out for us, we'd be taking them away for safe-keeping, on the acropolis, and putting an official seal on the door – just as we do with public gold,[51] only they'd be far more precious – to make sure nobody corrupted them, so that when they came of age they could be useful to their cities.

MENO: Yes, we probably would, Socrates.

c SOCRATES: So if good people aren't made good by their nature, is it learning that makes them good?

MENO: Yes, I'm now convinced that must be the answer. And besides, Socrates, going on our hypothesis, if we're sure being good is a form of knowledge, then it's obviously teachable.

SOCRATES: And maybe that's right. But then again . . . we may have been wrong to settle on it being knowledge.

MENO: What? But we thought that sounded right just a moment ago!

SOCRATES: Yes, but I'm afraid it's no good if it only seemed to be right a moment ago; it's also got to seem right *now*, and to keep on seeming right – otherwise it's worthless.

d MENO: So why the doubts about it being a form of knowledge? What's bothering you?

SOCRATES: Well, I'll tell you, Meno. You see, the claim that, if it's knowledge then it's teachable, I think is fine. I'm not taking that back. But as for it being knowledge – see if you think I'm not right to have my doubts. Tell me this: if something can be taught – not just how to be a good man but whatever – wouldn't there have to be people teaching it and people learning it?

MENO: Yes, I suppose so.

e SOCRATES: And conversely, if there's something that nobody teaches and nobody learns, then it's a pretty safe bet that it's something that can't be taught?

MENO: That's right. So . . . don't you think there are people who can teach us how to be good?

[*Anytus sits down beside Meno, listening to the conversation. Socrates notices him.*]

SOCRATES: Well, all I can say is, I've often asked that question: Are there people out there who can teach us about being good? And for the life of me, I can't find the answer. And yet

I'm always getting people to help me figure it out . . . especially anyone I think is a real expert on the subject . . . speaking of which, Meno, Anytus[52] here has joined us at just the right moment! Let's ask *him* to help us with our question. He'd be an ideal person to ask: for a start, he's the son of Anthemion – a wealthy and intelligent man; and Anthemion didn't get rich by any fluke, or from someone handing him his money on a plate (not like Ismenias the Theban, who just recently took Polycrates' bribe[53]); no, he made his wealth by his own brains and diligence[54]; and generally he's known for not being an uppity sort of citizen, or pompous and tiresome, but as a modest and unpretentious man. What's more, he did a very fine job of bringing up and educating Anytus here, in the view of the great Athenian public[55] – at any rate, they keep electing him to their highest public offices. So these are exactly the kind of men to help us figure out if there are people who can give lessons on being good – and if so, who?

90 a

b

[*He turns to Anytus.*] So, Anytus, I wonder if you could help us – myself and Meno here, your guest. We're trying to find out who the teachers are in this particular field. Now look at it like this: suppose we wanted Meno here to become a good doctor. Who would we send him to, to teach him? Doctors, presumably?

c

ANYTUS: Of course.

SOCRATES: And what if we wanted him to become good at making shoes? We'd send him off to the shoemakers, wouldn't we?

ANYTUS: Yes.

SOCRATES: And it's the same with everything else?

ANYTUS: Yes, of course.

SOCRATES: So tell me this (we'll use the same example): we're saying that if we wanted Meno here to become a doctor, we'd be doing the right thing by sending him to study with doctors. In saying that, don't we just mean that the sensible thing to do is to send him to the people who claim to have the relevant skill (rather than people who don't), and who charge a fee on exactly that basis, and publicly state that they can teach it to anyone who wants to come along and learn?

d

That's what we have in mind when we say they're the right people to send him to?

ANYTUS: Yes.

SOCRATES: Right. And the same goes for flute-playing and the
e      rest? It'd be really brainless, if we wanted someone to become a good flute player, to refuse to send him to the people who actually offer to teach the flute, and make a living out of it, and instead go and annoy some other bunch of people by expecting them to teach him* even though they make no pretence of being able to teach the thing we expect him to learn from them, and have never had a single student! Don't you think that would be pretty silly?

ANYTUS: Well, of course! You'd have to be a total idiot.

SOCRATES: I quite agree. So listen, then – we've got an oppor-
91 a    tunity here to put our heads together and try to decide what to do about young Meno, our visitor. The thing is, Anytus, Meno's been telling me all morning that what he wants is that particular kind of knowledge, that particular way of being good, that makes people run their households and their cities well, and look after their parents, and know how to welcome their guests (fellow-citizens or strangers) and help them on their way, as a good man should. So if he wants to
b      be good in that sense, the question is: who should we send him to? Or is it obvious, going by what we've just said? Presumably we should send him to the people who actually offer lessons on being good, and advertise their courses as open to any Greek who wants to learn, and charge a fixed rate for the service?

ANYTUS: And who're they, Socrates? Who do you mean?

SOCRATES: Surely you must know who I mean – I'm talking about the people they call 'sophists'.

c   ANYTUS: Holy Herakles! What a shocking suggestion,⁵⁶ Socrates! I hope no relative or friend of mine, Athenian or foreigner, is ever crazy enough to go to those people and submit to their abuse! Because that's all those people are – blatant abusers and corrupters of anyone who associates with them!

SOCRATES: Really, Anytus? So, that makes them *unique* among

people who claim expertise at providing services: so utterly
unlike all the rest that instead of improving what you place
in their care (like the others), they do the opposite – they
mess it up! And then they have the nerve to expect to be    d
paid? I really don't know if I can believe you. I know of a
single man, Protagoras, who made more money as a sophist
than Phidias[57] – who created such wonderfully beautiful
works of art – and any ten other sculptors put together. So
what you're suggesting is miraculous. I mean, if people
who mended old shoes or patched up old cloaks gave them
back in a worse state than they got them, they wouldn't    e
get away with it for thirty days. They'd soon find themselves starving. So how on earth can Protagoras have fooled
the whole of Greece and got away with corrupting his
pupils – sending them away more depraved than when he
took them on – for more than forty *years*? That's right, I
think he was around seventy years old when he died, and he
practised his profession for forty years, and throughout that
time, and to this day, he's carried on being very highly
regarded. And there've been a whole lot of other sophists
besides Protagoras; some before his time and some who are    92 a
still alive today. Now, if what you're saying is true, what are
we supposed to think? That they're *deliberately* duping
and abusing young people? Or that even they don't realize
what they're doing? Is it plausible they could be that crazy –
these men who some people say are the finest minds of their
day?

ANYTUS: No, they're far from being crazy, Socrates. I'll tell you
who's crazy: the young men who give these people money.
And their families are even crazier for letting them. And    b
craziest of all are the cities that let them in instead of sending
them packing – and that goes for anyone who tries that sort
of thing, whether he's a foreigner or a local.[58]

SOCRATES: Have any of the sophists ever personally done you
any harm, Anytus? Why are you so hard on them?

ANYTUS: Certainly not. I've never had any dealings with any
sophist, and I'd never let anyone else in my family associate
with one, either.

SOCRATES: So, in fact, you have absolutely no first-hand experience of them whatsoever?

ANYTUS: And I hope it stays that way.

c SOCRATES: But in that case – I'm a little puzzled – how can you be so sure about something you've got absolutely no experience of? How can you know what's good or bad about it?

ANYTUS: Easily! I certainly know what *those* people are, whether I've had first-hand experience or not.

SOCRATES: Perhaps you're a soothsayer, Anytus. How else you manage to know about these men, from what you say yourself, is a mystery. But it really doesn't matter, because in any case we weren't trying to find out who Meno should go

d to for lessons in depravity. (Let's say that's the sophists, if you like.) No, tell us about the right people: help out your old family friend[59] here by explaining who he should go and see, in this great city of ours, to become a man renowned for being good in the sense I outlined a moment ago.

ANYTUS: Why don't you just tell him yourself?

SOCRATES: I did. I just said who I thought could teach that kind of thing; but it turns out I'm talking nonsense – according to

e you, and you're probably right. So it's your turn. You tell him which people in Athens he should go and see. Give him a name – any name.

ANYTUS: I don't see why we need to name anyone in particular. The fact is, any decent[60] Athenian he meets, every single one, will make him a better man than sophists ever could, as long as he follows his advice.

SOCRATES: And how did these 'decent' people get to be decent? All on their own? Without learning anything from anyone? How can they teach people something they never learned

93 a themselves?

ANYTUS: I expect they learned from the generation before them, who were equally decent men. Or don't you think this city has had plenty of good men in its time?

SOCRATES: Oh, yes, I do, Anytus, I do. I think there are good men in Athens today – good on civic and ethical matters –

and yes, there've been good men in the past as well. But
here's the thing: Were they also good at teaching what it was
that made them good? Because that's what we're talking
about here. The question isn't whether or not there are any
good men in Athens, or whether there've been any good men
in the past, but whether being good is something that can be   b
taught – that's what we've spent all this time looking into.
And that means that what we're really asking is this: Is it the
case that good men, today, or in the past, knew how to pass
on to other people what it was that made them good? Or is
it something that can't be passed on or handed over from
one person to another? That's what Meno and I have spent
so long trying to figure out.

So think about it like this, going on what you just said
yourself: Do you think Themistocles[61] was a good man?          c

ANYTUS: Yes. Outstandingly.

SOCRATES: And do you also think he was good at teaching
what it was that made him a good man? If anyone could, he
could, right?

ANYTUS: Yes, I assume so – if he wanted to.

SOCRATES: Well, wouldn't he have wanted to? Wouldn't he
have wanted his own son – to give only the most obvious
example – to become a decent man? Or do you think he was
a stingy father and deliberately refused to pass on what it
was that made him good? Haven't you heard the stories       d
about Themistocles and his son, Cleophantus? He certainly
had him taught to be a good horseman. Apparently the boy
could ride a horse standing up – stand upright and throw
javelins as he rode – and do all sorts of other amazing things
that his father had him taught and made him expert at:
everything that called for good teachers. Or haven't you
heard those stories from your grandparents?

ANYTUS: Yes, I have.

SOCRATES: So no one could have accused his son of lacking
natural ability?[62]

ANYTUS: Maybe not.                                              e

SOCRATES: What about this, then: Have you ever heard anyone,

young or old, say that Cleophantus, Themistocles' son, was
a good man, like his father, with the kind of knowledge his
father had?

ANYTUS: Hardly.

SOCRATES: So what are we to think – that he was keen to teach
him those other things, yet when it came to his own kind of
knowledge, didn't want to make his own son any better than
the next man (assuming, that is, that being a good man was
something teachable)?

ANYTUS: It certainly doesn't seem likely.

SOCRATES: So that's Themistocles for you, then: hopeless at
teaching people how to be good – and yet you agree he was
one of the very best men there's been. So let's take a look at
94 a     another one: Aristides.[63] You agree he was a good man?

ANYTUS: Yes, absolutely.

SOCRATES: Right; and isn't it the same story? In all the areas
that called for teachers, he gave his son, Lysimachus,[64] the
finest education in Athens; but did he make him a better man
than anyone else? What do you think? You must have met
him; you've seen what he's like. Or how about Pericles – a
b     man of such abundant wisdom! – you know that he raised
two sons, Paralus and Xanthippus?

ANYTUS: Yes.

SOCRATES: Well, as you know yourself, he trained those boys
to be the best horsemen in Athens; and he had them trained
to be second to none in music, and athletics, and everything
that calls for professional teaching. So it's hardly likely that
he didn't also want to make them good men. No, I think he
wanted to, all right; the problem, I suspect, is that it just can't
be taught. And consider the case of Thucydides[65] – because I
wouldn't want you to think it's only these few, very *unim-
pressive*, Athenians who've been incompetent in this respect!
c     Thucydides brought up two sons as well, Stephanus and
Melesias, and apart from him giving them a good all-round
education, they could wrestle better than anyone in Athens
(he sent one of them to Xanthias and the other one to
Eudorus, and those two were known as the finest wrestlers
of their day) – remember?

ANYTUS: Yes, so I've heard.

SOCRATES: Right; and obviously there's no way he'd have spent
so much money on those expensive forms of teaching for his    d
boys, and yet not bothered to turn them into good men, when
he could have taught them that *at no expense at all* – that is,
if it was teachable. Or was Thucydides just some ordinary
man? Didn't he have loads of friends, both in Athens and
among the allies?[66] He was from a leading aristocratic family
and a very influential man, here and in the rest of Greece. So
if it was something teachable at all, he'd surely have found
someone who could turn his boys into good men – either
someone here in Athens or a foreigner – even if he didn't
have time to do it himself because he was too busy taking    e
care of the city's affairs. No, Anytus, my friend, it looks like
being good simply can't be taught.

ANYTUS: Socrates, it seems to me you're rather casual about
badmouthing people. Personally, I'd advise you to watch
your back,[67] if you know what's good for you. I don't know
if it's the same in other cities, but it's certainly the case in
this one that it's easier to do people harm than it is to do
them good. But I assume you already know that.              95 a

[*Anytus leaves the conversation, but stays within sight of
Socrates and Meno.*]

SOCRATES: I get the feeling Anytus is a bit angry with me,
Meno; and I'm not surprised. It's because he thinks I'm being
rude about those men – plus the fact that he sees himself as
one of them. Well, one day he may find out what it really
means to badmouth a man,[68] and then he'll stop being angry.
For now, he has no idea.

Now tell me; don't you have good, decent men up there in
Thessaly, as well?

MENO: Absolutely.

SOCRATES: So are they prepared to offer themselves as teachers    b
to the young? Do they all agree that being good is something
teachable, and that they're the ones to teach it?

MENO: No, not at all, Socrates. Sometimes you'll hear them claim it's teachable, and then sometimes they'll claim it isn't teachable.

SOCRATES: Well, if they can't even agree about that, we can hardly say that this is something that they teach, can we?

MENO: No, I suppose not, Socrates.

SOCRATES: Well, what about these 'sophists', then – the only people who make it their profession? What's your view? Do you think they can teach us about being good?

c MENO: That's what most impresses me about Gorgias,[69] Socrates – the fact that you'll never hear him claiming to make people good. In fact, he even scoffs at other sophists when he hears them make that sort of claim. He thinks their job is just to make people skilled at public speaking.

SOCRATES: So in other words you don't think sophists can teach it either?

MENO: I can't quite decide, Socrates. I feel the same way about it as most people do. Sometimes I think they can, sometimes I think they can't.

SOCRATES: You know that you political men aren't the only ones who can't make up your minds about whether or not d it's teachable? You know the poet Theognis[70] says exactly the same?

MENO: Really? Where?

SOCRATES: In that elegiac poem where first he says,

> Always wine with, and dine with, and try to get in with
>     the people with plenty of power.
> From good men you'll be taught what a decent man ought.
>     Never mingle with men who are bad.
> If you're in the wrong crowd, you will rapidly lose
> e     every single good notion you had.

You realize that here he's talking as if being good is something that can be taught?

MENO: He certainly seems to be.

SOCRATES: But then in a different bit of the poem, he's rather changed his tune:

You know, if it were true, that good sense could be *made*,
    and then simply installed in a man . . .

he says (or something like that), then the people who could
'install' it . . .

    would be rich; they'd be raking it in . . .

and what's more, if that were so . . .

    Then explain how the child of a man who was good
    ever came to be worse than his dad.
    He got plenty of solid advice. It's not so:                    96 a
    teaching *won't* turn you good, if you're bad.

You see? He's talking about exactly the same thing, and
contradicting himself.

MENO: Apparently.

SOCRATES: So can you name any other thing where the people
   who claim to teach it,[71] so far from being acknowledged as
   capable of teaching anyone else, aren't even recognized as
   knowing anything about it themselves – they're actually
   thought to be especially bad at the very thing they claim to    b
   teach![72] – meanwhile, the people who are acknowledged as
   decent men themselves can't make up their minds about
   whether or not it can be taught? And if they're so confused
   about it, do you think they could possibly be teaching it
   properly?

MENO: Absolutely not.

SOCRATES: So if sophists can't teach it, and people who are
   decent men themselves can't teach it, clearly nobody else
   could be teaching it?

MENO: No. I don't think so.

SOCRATES: And if nobody's teaching it, then nobody's learning  c
   it, either?

MENO: That's right.

SOCRATES: And we already agreed that if there's something

that nobody teaches, and nobody learns, then it's something
that can't be taught?

MENO: Yes, we did.

SOCRATES: And there's no trace, anywhere, of anyone teaching
people how to be good?

MENO: Right.

SOCRATES: And if there's no one teaching it, there's no one
learning it?

MENO: Apparently not.

SOCRATES: So it looks like being good is something that can't
be taught?

d   MENO: It looks that way – if we've thought it through correctly;
which makes me wonder, Socrates, if maybe there aren't even
any good men at all! Or, how on earth *do* people become
good, if and when they do?

SOCRATES: Chances are, Meno, you and I are a couple of rather
ordinary men. I'm afraid our teachers – Gorgias in your case,
and in my case, Prodicus[73] – haven't educated us well enough.
So we've definitely got to take a good look at ourselves and
find out who's going to make us better, somehow or other.

e   And I'm saying that with this search of ours in mind: what
idiots we've been! How silly of us not to realize that it isn't
always *knowledge* that's guiding people when they do things
well and succeed in their affairs. That's probably why the
answer keeps getting away from us – I mean, the discovery
of how exactly good men become good.

MENO: How do you mean, Socrates?

SOCRATES: Here's what I mean. We were right to agree that
97 a   men who *are* good also always *do* good – weren't we?[74]
That's got to be right?

MENO: Yes.

SOCRATES: And we were also right to agree that good men will
do us good if they guide us in our affairs and 'show us the
way'?[75]

MENO: Yes.

SOCRATES: But the claim that you can only show people the
way if you have wisdom – it looks like we were wrong to
agree on that.

MENO: What makes you say that?

SOCRATES: Well, I'll tell you. Look – suppose someone *knew* the way to Larissa (or wherever) and was on his way there, and showing other people how to get there; obviously he'd be good at showing them the right way?

MENO: Of course.

SOCRATES: And what about someone who had an *opinion* on    b how to get there – a correct opinion – but who'd never actually been there, and didn't know how to get there; wouldn't he be able to show them the way as well?

MENO: Of course.

SOCRATES: And presumably as long as he has his correct opinion (about the same thing the other man has knowledge of), he'll be every bit as good at showing people the way? With his true belief, but without knowledge, he'll be just as good a guide as the man with the knowledge?

MENO: Yes, he'll be just as good.

SOCRATES: In other words, true opinion is just as good a guide to right action as knowledge. There's the key fact that we kept leaving out, just now, when we were looking into the nature of being good. We said that wisdom was the only thing that can show us how to do things the right way. But    c that's not so. There's also true opinion.

MENO: Yes, it certainly looks like it.

SOCRATES: So in other words, a correct opinion does just as much good as knowledge?

MENO: Except in one respect, Socrates. If you have knowledge, then you'll *always* be dead on target; but if you only have a correct opinion, sometimes you'll hit, and sometimes you'll miss.

SOCRATES: What makes you say that? If you've always got the correct opinion, won't you always be 'on target' as long as you've got your correct opinion?

MENO: Yes, good point ... it seems that must be right; which leaves me wondering, Socrates: If that's the case, why on earth is knowledge so much more valuable than cor-    d rect opinion, and why are they treated as two different things?

SOCRATES: Well, you know why it is you're wondering about it? Shall I tell you?

MENO: Go ahead.

SOCRATES: It's because you haven't pondered Daedalus' statues.[76] Maybe you haven't even got any up there in Thessaly.

MENO: What have they got to do with it?

SOCRATES: Well, they're the same: if they aren't shackled, they escape – they scamper away. But if they're shackled, they stay put.

e MENO: What are you getting at?

SOCRATES: If you own an original Daedalus, unshackled, it's not worth all that much – like a slave who keeps running away – because it doesn't stay put. But if you've got one that's shackled, it's very valuable. Because they're really lovely pieces of work. What am I getting at? My point is, it's the same with true opinions. True opinions, as long as they stay put, are a fine thing and do us a whole lot of good.

98 a Only, they tend not to stay put for very long. They're always scampering away from a person's soul. So they're not very valuable until you shackle them by figuring out what makes them true.[77] (And that, my dear Meno, is a matter of remembering, as we agreed earlier.) And then, once they're shackled, they turn into knowledge, and become stable and fixed. So that's why knowledge is a more valuable thing than correct opinion, and that's how knowledge *differs* from a correct opinion: by a shackle.

MENO: You know, I bet that's pretty much right, Socrates.

b SOCRATES: Of course, I'm speaking as someone who doesn't have knowledge myself. I'm just guessing. But I certainly don't think it's only a guess that correct opinion and knowledge are two very different things. If there's anything at all I'd claim to know – and I wouldn't claim to know a lot – I'd certainly count that as one of the things I know for sure.

MENO: And you're quite right to, Socrates.

SOCRATES: So tell me: Am I also right in saying that if true opinion is guiding you, it's just as good as knowledge at achieving the goal of any sort of action?

MENO: Yes, I think that's right as well.

SOCRATES: So correct opinion is just as good a thing as know-   c
ledge and does us just as much good in our actions; and a
man with correct opinions will do as much good as a man
with knowledge?

MENO: Right.

SOCRATES: And we agreed that that was a characteristic of a
good man – doing good?

MENO: Yes.

SOCRATES: So it isn't just knowledge that makes men good,
and able to do their cities good, if and when they do; it's also
correct opinion. In which case, given that neither one of those
things – knowledge or true opinion – arises in people just by   d
nature . . . or am I wrong about that? Do you think either of
them comes to us naturally?

MENO: No.

SOCRATES: So if neither of them comes naturally, it can't be
people's nature that makes them good men?

MENO: No, it can't be.

SOCRATES: And since our nature doesn't make us good . . . the
next thing we asked[78] was whether being good is something
teachable?

MENO: Yes.

SOCRATES: Right, and didn't we decide that being good is
teachable *if* it's a kind of wisdom?

MENO: Yes.

SOCRATES: And conversely, that it would have to be a kind of
wisdom, if it's teachable?

MENO: Exactly.

SOCRATES: And that if there are people teaching it, then it's   e
teachable; but if there aren't any people teaching it, then it
isn't teachable?

MENO: That's right.

SOCRATES: And we've decided that there aren't any people
teaching it?

MENO: We did.

SOCRATES: So that means we've decided that it isn't teachable,
and that it isn't a kind of wisdom?

MENO: Exactly.

SOCRATES: But we're certainly agreeing that it's a good thing?

MENO: Yes.

SOCRATES: And that what's good – what does us good – is the element that guides us and shows us the right way?

MENO: Absolutely.

99 a SOCRATES: And that there are only two things that can show us the right way: true opinion and knowledge. At least, that's what a person has to have, to show the way. I don't count things that come out right just by some stroke of luck. That's not a case of anything happening through human guidance. In any area where people show the way, those are the only possible guides: true opinion and knowledge.

MENO: I think that's right.

SOCRATES: And since being good is something that can't be taught, it's no longer an option that it's knowledge?

MENO: Apparently not.

b SOCRATES: So of the only two things that are good, and that enable us to do good, that rules out knowledge: it seems it isn't knowledge that guides people in the civic and ethical sphere.

MENO: I agree.

SOCRATES: So in other words it wasn't through having knowledge, or by being experts, that men like that were able to guide their cities – men like Themistocles and the ones Anytus was talking about. Of course! That's why they couldn't turn other people into the sort of men they were themselves – because it wasn't knowledge that made them the way they were.

MENO: That seems very plausible, Socrates.

SOCRATES: So if it wasn't knowledge that made them the way they were, the only remaining possibility is that it was a sort

c of knack for having the right opinions. That's what statesmen must use to set their cities on the right path; and that means they're just like fortune-tellers and soothsayers,[79] in terms of how close they are to having knowledge. Soothsayers are the same: when they're 'inspired', they say plenty of things that are true; but they don't really know what they're saying.

MENO: Yes, that's probably right.

SOCRATES: And isn't it right to call people 'inspired' when they achieve lots of great things by what they say and do, without any understanding?

MENO: Absolutely.

SOCRATES: So it makes sense to call those people inspired: the fortune-tellers and soothsayers; and poets and playwrights, too; and we'd be especially right to call statesmen inspired, and to say they're in a kind of trance, possessed by some divine spirit, when they achieve so many great successes by saying the things they say, even though they don't really know what they're talking about.

MENO: Absolutely.

SOCRATES: And remember that women, Meno, call good men 'inspired'; and in Sparta, too, the highest praise for a good man is when they say, 'That man's *inzpired.*'*[80]

MENO: And apparently they're right, Socrates. Mind you, Anytus here will probably get annoyed* with you for saying so.

SOCRATES: I don't care about that. We'll talk with him again[81] some other time, Meno. As for us, here and now – if we've done a good job of our search for the truth, and if what we've said at each stage of our talk was right, then it turns out that being good is not something that comes to us naturally, or something that can be taught; instead, it seems it arises by gift of god, and without understanding, in the people who have it ... unless, that is, there were a man,[82] among good statesmen, who could also turn someone else into the sort of man he is himself. If there were such a man, they'd probably speak of him as being up here among the living just what Homer says Tiresias was among the dead. He says,

> He alone has sense in the world below;[83]
> the rest are flitting shadows.

A man like that would be the same thing here: something real, among mere shadows of what it is to be good.

MENO: I think that's quite right, and very nicely put, Socrates.

SOCRATES: So by our line of reasoning, Meno, it appears that being good is a quality that comes to people, when it does, by gift of god. Of course, we really won't know for sure until we set aside the question of exactly how it comes to people and first try to find out what being good is, in itself.

But now it's time for me to go. And as for you, try to convince your host Anytus here about the things you've been convinced about yourself – try to calm him down. If you can do that, you may well be doing Athens a favour.[84]

# Appendix

This translation follows Burnet's text of both the *Protagoras* and the *Meno*, except in the following few places. Most of these slight changes come from other editors (four, in the case of the *Meno*, I take from Bluck); none is of any philosophical importance, except perhaps *Protagoras* 355d, where, although I am not happy with Burnet's text, I still follow the majority view as to the basic sense of the sentence.

| BURNET | THIS TRANSLATION |
|---|---|
| **Protagoras** | |
| **309c5**: ξένω (misprint) | ξένῳ |
| **311b1**: ἀποπειρώμενος...τῆς ῥώμης | ἀποπειρώμενος...τῆς γνώμης |
| **312e3**: — Δῆλον ὅτι... (*Hippocrates*) | δῆλον ὅτι... (*Socrates*), or ἢ δῆλον ὅτι... |
| **312e4**: — Εἰκός γε. τί δή ἐστιν... (*Soc.*) (with last, probably a printer's error) | — Εἰκός γε. (*Hipp.*) — Τί δή ἐστιν... (*Soc.*) (as in all other editions) |
| **323b7**: [δικαιοσύνην] | δικαιοσύνην |
| **323d6**: τὰ καλά | τὰ κακά |
| **331c2**: ἐν αὐτῷ | ἐν αὐτοῖν |
| **338b4**: αἰσχρὸν εἴη | αἰσχρὸν ἂν εἴη |
| **339a3**: διελεῖν | διελθεῖν |
| **342c8**: καὶ αὐτοὶ οὐδένα | καὶ διὰ τοῦτ' οὐδένα |
| **348d2**: πως | οὕτως |

| BURNET | THIS TRANSLATION |
|---|---|
| **355d4**: ἐν ὑμῖν | I delete ἐν ὑμῖν. It may mean 'in your view', but that seems very unusual. There are various possible emendations. |
| **356d4**: αὕτη μὲν ἡμᾶς ἐπλάνα | αὕτη μὲν ἂν ἡμᾶς ἐπλάνα |
| **359d2**: ἢ ἐπὶ τὰ μή; | μᾶλλον ἢ ἐπὶ τὰ μή; (perhaps ἐξὸν ἐπὶ τὰ μή;) |

## Meno

| | |
|---|---|
| **73d3**: ἄρχειν οἵω τε εἶναι | ἄρχειν οἵου τε εἶναι |
| **75d6**: ὧν ἂν προσομολογῇ εἰδέναι ὁ ἐρωτώμενος. | ὧν ἅτερος ὁμολογεῖ εἰδέναι ἐρωτώμενος. |
| **79b7**: τί οὖν δὴ τοῦτο λέγω; ὅτι... (Soc.) | ΜΕΝ. Τί οὖν δή; ΣΩ. Τοῦτο λέγω, ὅτι... |
| **81a1**: Οὐκοῦν | Οὔκουν |
| **84e4**: Οὐκοῦν ἐστιν αὕτη γραμμὴ ἐκ γωνίας εἰς γωνίαν [τινὰ] τέμνουσα... | Οὐκοῦν ἔστιν αὖ τοιαύτη γραμμή, ἐκ γωνίας εἰς γωνίαν τέμνουσα... |
| **86a8**: ἀρ' οὖν | ἀρ' οὐ |
| **90e4**: ζητοῦντα μανθάνειν | ἀξιοῦντας μανθάνειν |
| **94c4**: ἐπάλαισαν | ἐπάλαιον (or ἐπαλαιέτην with τούτω in c2) (Aristippus: *palestizabant*) |
| **99d9**: Θεῖος | Σεῖος |
| **99e2**: ἄχθεται | ἀχθέσεται |

# Glossary

This Glossary lists some of the important words and phrases used in the two dialogues. It is aimed at students of ancient philosophy who are reading other Greek texts and works of scholarship on those texts, as well as at people learning ancient Greek. It shows how I have translated some of the key terms, and gives various other possible translations in each case and, where applicable, the traditional translations, which are widely used. The words in bold on the left (in Greek) all appear in the *Protagoras* or the *Meno* (or in both). On the right, the words or phrases in italics are the ones actually used in this version; the others are other ways in which the terms have been, or might be, translated (in the Greek of this period, dialect and context), including the traditional terminology. Only a small number of terms are unambiguously part of the latter category; for the great majority of these words there has always been variation in how they are translated. Translations also marked with an asterisk are ones that I myself consider to be inaccurate. The accents marked on the transliterated Greek words are a very approximate guide to pronunciation: they may be treated as marking the stressed syllable of the words. I have not distinguished between long and short vowels.

**agathós** (1) *good*, i.e. *a good man*; *good person* (2) *good at* [something]; *a good* [something, e.g. carpenter]
**(ta) agathá** (1) *good things*; *things that are good for us* (2) *the good things* [under discussion]
– **(ta) kaká** (1) *bad things*; *things that are bad for us* (2) *the bad things* [under discussion]; *evils**
**ágnoia** *ignorance*; [state of] *not knowing*

**aidós** (poetic/archaic term) feeling of shame; reverance; embarrassment; *sense of wrong*

**amathía** *ignorance*; stupidity

**anámnesis** *remembering* (n.); recollection

– **anamnesthénai** *to remember*; to recollect

– **anamnestón** [something that] can be remembered; *rememberable*; recollectable

**andreíos** *brave*; courageous

**andreía** (1) *bravery*; *being brave*; courage (2) *enthusiasm*; energy

**aphrosúnë** *foolishness*; *stupidity*; *being stupid*; folly

**aporeín** (1) to have no means (2) metaphorically: *to have no idea what to do*; to have no clue; *to be puzzled*; *to be baffled*; to be perplexed

**aporía** (1) lack of means; poverty; [state of] having no means or provisions (2) used as opposite of **póros**: non-getting; [instance of] *not acquiring anything* (3) metaphorically: [state of] having no clue, no means or way of finding the answer; hence [state of] being clueless, *being baffled*; *bafflement*; *puzzlement*; perplexity

**areté** (see **agathós**) (a) general: (1) *being good*, i.e. the state/quality of being good, esp. of *being a good man*; *being a good person*; goodness; virtue; excellence* (2) *being a good* [something, e.g. carpenter]; being good at [something] (see below); virtue*; excellence. [Use (2) is rare; there are three examples in the *Protagoras*, none in the *Meno*.] (b) particular: *way/form/manner of being good*; hence a good quality, esp. of character, i.e. an ethical quality; a virtue. [In the *Meno* only.]

– **andrós areté** *being a good man*; man's virtue; manly virtue

– **gunaikós areté** *being a good woman*; woman's virtue

– **politiké areté** *being a good citizen*; civic virtue; political virtue*

– **areté tektoniké** *being a good carpenter*; skill as a carpenter*

– **aretés didáskaloi** teachers of being good; teachers of virtue; *people who can teach* [us] *how to be good/about being good*

– **didaktón he areté** *being good can be taught/is teachable*; *you can make people good by teaching them*

– **mía areté** *one* [*idea of*] *being good*; single/universal [concept of] being good; one virtue; single virtue

– **mórion aretés** *part of being good*; part of virtue [often used as an equivalent to 'particular' **areté**]

– **ten aretén paradidónai** to pass on/hand over [the quality of] being good; *to pass on what it is that makes you good*; to impart virtue; to bestow virtue

– **tí estin areté?** *what is being good?*; what is virtue?

**aulós** *flute*; mijwiz; arghoul

**deilía** *cowardice*; being a coward

**deilós** *a coward*; cowardly

**dialégesthai** *to talk*; *to talk* [things/something] *through*; *to have a conversation or discussion*

**dialektikóteron** more talk-through-ishly; *in a more talk-it-through kind of way*; more dialectically (coined by Plato)

**diálogos** a *talk*; a *discussion*; a talking through; a dialogue; a conversation

**díkaion** *right*; ethical; just

– **ádikon** *wrong*; unethical; unjust (action)

**dikaíos** (δικαίως) *according to what's right*; *rightfully*; ethically; justly

– **adíkos** (ἀδίκως) *wrongfully*; unethically; unjustly

**díkaios** (δίκαιος) *ethical* [person]; [*someone who*] *cares about what's right*; someone who does what's right; righteous; just (person)

– **ádikos** (ἄδικος) wrongdoer; *criminal*; unethical; unjust [person]

**dikaiosúnë** *respect for what's right*; *doing what's right*; [state of] being righteous; [state of] *being ethical*; righteousness; morality; justice*

– **adikía** *disregard for what's right*; injustice*; wrongdoing; unrighteousness; immorality; [state of] being unethical

– **adikeín** (1) *to do wrong*; *to wrong* [someone]; to commit an injustice (2) *to commit a crime*

**díkë** (poetic/archaic term) right (n.); righteousness; *sense of right*

**dóxa** *opinion*; belief; view; what you think is the case

– **dóxa alethés** *true opinion*; true belief

– **orthé dóxa** *correct opinion*; correct belief (= previous)

**epimeleía** *care*; concern; *care and effort*; *care and attention*; *diligence*

– **aretés epimeleísthai** *to care about being good*

**epistémë** *knowledge*

**(ta) hedéa** *pleasurable things*; *things that are pleasurable*

**hedoné** *pleasure*

– **hettásthai hupó ton hedonón** lit. to be defeated by pleasures (?); *to be unable to resist pleasures*; to be overcome by pleasures

– **to hettó eínai ton hedonón** lit. to be less than pleasures; *to be unable to resist pleasures*; to be overcome by pleasure (= previous)

**hegeísthai** to lead; *to guide*; *to show the way*

– **hegeísthai orthós** to guide right; *to show the right way*; *to show the way* (i.e., by implication, the right way)

**hósion** (of things/actions) *required by religion*; permitted by religion; pious; holy; halal

– **anósion** (of things/actions) *against religion*; irreligious; unholy; impious; sinful; haram; heinous

**hósios** (of people) *religious* [person]; pious; holy

**hosiótës** *being religious; religiousness;* piety; holiness

**kakía** *being bad;* badness; vice (opposite of areté)

**kalós, kalón** (1) *beautiful;* fine (in old sense) (2) *honourable;* ethical; *noble;* ethically acceptable; fair; right; *fine* (modern sense); okay

– **aischrós, aischrón** (1) *ugly* (2) disgraceful; *shameful;* unethical; *wrong;* reprehensible; unacceptable; foul* (3) *insulting;* shaming

**kalós k'agathós** *good and decent* [man]; *decent;* a gentleman

**kithára** *guitar;* lyre; krar

**lógos** (1) a thing said/claimed; a *claim;* an *idea;* a proposition (2) an *argument* (3) a *speech* (4) an account (5) reason; rationality

**lúpe** *pain*

– **ta luperá** (= ta aniará) *painful things; things that are painful*

**manthánein** *to learn*

**máthesis** *learning* (n.)

– **mathetón** *learnable*

– **didaktón** *teachable; can be taught*

**nárke** *numbfish;* electric ray; torpedo fish

**opheleín** *to do* [someone, us] *good; to benefit*

**ophélimon** [something that] *does us good;* good for us; *beneficial;* esp. in very broad sense: [something that] *does us good in life*

**ophélimos** [a person who] *does good;* beneficent; beneficial

**phrónesis** understanding, esp. of practical and ethical kind; *wisdom;* prudence; practical wisdom

**phrónimos** *wise;* prudent

**pólis** *city; society;* state

– **ta tes póleos** city stuff; *affairs of the city; public matters*

**polítes** (1) *citizen* (2) fellow-citizen; *fellow countryman*

– **ta politiká** citizens' stuff; civic affairs; *the city's affairs; civic and ethical matters;* politics

– **politiké areté** *being a good citizen;* civic virtue; political virtue*; political excellence*

– **politiké práxis** civic activity; civic action; *the civic and ethical sphere* [of action]

– **politiké téchne** citizen's know-how/skill/craft; *civic and ethical know-how; ethical know-how;* political art*; the art of politics*; the art of citizenship; knack of living as fellow-citizens

– **politikós** *statesman;* politician; *political man*

– **sképsasthai** *to look at;* always metaphorical, in sense of *to look into; to investigate;* to examine

– **diasképsasthai** *to look into thoroughly; to get to the bottom of; to investigate*

**sophía** (1) *knowledge; expertise;* the [state of] *having knowledge;*

[state of] *being expert*; wisdom\* (2) *intelligence*; cleverness (3) *philosophy*

**sophístës** public intellectual; professional philosopher; *sophist*

**sophós** (1) (colloquial) *clever; smart; intelligent*; skilled; wise\* (2) *knowing* (adj.); knowledgeable (3) (as a noun) *an intellectual; an expert*; a wise man\*

**sóphron** *sensible*; moderate; restrained; temperate\*

**sophroneín** *to be sensible; to act sensibly* (i.e. (1) to be moderate (2) to be reasonable/rational); to act temperately\*

**sophrosúnë** [state of] *being sensible; good sense; moderation; self-control* (at *Meno* 88b); temperance\*

**sumphorá** event; disaster; catastrophe; a *tough break*

– **améchanos sumphorá** a tough break that there is no way of coping with; a *tough break that beats every move you make*

**tharreín** *to be unafraid* [of something]; *not to be afraid of* [something]; to be confident\*

– **phobeísthai** *to be afraid* [of something]; to fear

– **ta tharraléa** (= ta me deiná) *things that are not frightening*; things that are [objectively] not frightening; *things you should not be afraid of*

– **ta deiná** *things that are frightening*; things that are [objectively] frightening; *things you should be afraid of*

– **hoi tharraléoi** *people who are not afraid*; the confident

– **thársos, thárros** *lack of fear; fearlessness*; boldness; confidence

**zeteín** (1) to search; to look for; *to try to find* (2) metaphorically: to look for an answer to a question; *to try to find out* [something]

– **zetetikós** *eager to find out* [things]; try-to-find-out-ish (coined by Plato)

# Notes

## PROTAGORAS

1. *There you are, Socrates*: In a public place, Socrates meets a friend (or friends) to whom he narrates the conversation he has just had with Protagoras. This outer dialogue lets Plato insert descriptive and dramatic detail (in the form of Socrates' commentary as narrator).

2. *Alcibiades*: Alcibiades (*c.* 450–404 BC) was the ward of Pericles, talented, charismatic and famously beautiful. He had a spectacular but chequered political career. It is a running theme in Plato's dialogues that Socrates is in love with him (see *Symposium* 212d–23b, *Gorgias* 481d, *Alcibiades I* 103a), as is implied here by the unnamed friend. Plato depicts their relationship in detail in the *Symposium* and is at pains to *deny* that it was conventional (i.e. sexual).

3. *the charm of youth*: Quoted from *Iliad* 24.348 and *Odyssey* 10.279. The friend's point was that since Alcibiades is growing his first beard, he is past the age of being a suitable object of male desire.

4. *boy*: A slave, *not* a boy. See note on the slave in the *Meno* (at 82b).

5. *Hippocrates ... Apollodoros ... Phason*: Probably real people but otherwise unknown to us. Hippocrates is a young and ambitious Athenian drawn to the teachings of the sophists, especially the training they offered in public speaking, which was such a valuable tool in public life in democratic Athens. His horsey name ('Hippocrates' means, roughly, 'horsepower') is very upper-class.

6. *banging on the door*: Scenes that open with frantic door-banging are a trademark of Greek comedies (see, e.g., Aristophanes' *Clouds* 132, *Acharnians* 394, *Peace* 178, *Frogs* 37, 460). There

are various allusions to comic drama in the *Protagoras*. The opening recalls *The Clouds* in particular, the play in which the main character wakes his son up very early in the morning and urges him to enrol with the crazy sophist, Socrates. In the *Protagoras*, Hippocrates wakes Socrates up early in the morning because he wants to enrol with the sophist Protagoras. Socrates' role is precisely reversed in what follows, so that the *Protagoras* is a kind of anti-*Clouds*. In other ways, the dialogue mimics Aristophanes' most famous play, *The Frogs* (see n. 20). Even the traditional subtitle of the dialogue (*The Sophists*) imitates comedy titles (*The Acharnians, The Knights, The Birds* etc.), although we do not know exactly where or when that subtitle originated.

7.  *camp-bed*: I.e. a *skimpous*; like an Indian charpoy, a web of netting on four stubby legs. Socrates was known for his asceticism. In *Clouds* (254) he is mocked for his *skimpous* in particular.

8.  *my boy, Satyros, ran away*: This is the only time Plato ever gives a (fictional) slave a name, so it seems likely that there is some point to it. 'Satyros' is a name connected with Socrates: in the *Symposium*, (215–17) Alcibiades says that Socrates resembles a *satyros* (a satyr) both physically and in his disrespectful cheekiness. The name is also connected with comedy: one genre of comedy was the satyr-play (in which satyrs made up the chorus). Perhaps Socrates is being assigned a comic role: 'My Satyr ran away, so I came to you.'

9.  *give him some money*: Sophists charged for tuition. The dialogue is full of disparaging references to this practice (here, 313c, 328b, 349a, 357e). Plato's characters often imply that there is something vulgar about earning money. Sophists were not independently wealthy, and their professionalism was a mark of their social origin. The stratification of society, and the existence of slavery in particular, made labour, and by extension wage-earning, socially unacceptable for elite Athenians.

10. *Callias, Hipponicus' son*: a very wealthy young aristocrat who was an enthusiastic fan and generous patron of sophists (see *Apology* 20a).

11. *Hippocrates blushed*: It is his aristocratic horror at the thought of earning a living by a 'profession' (see n. 9) that makes his admiration for sophists a very different matter from wanting to be one, rather as Victorian aristocrats used to worship actresses while regarding them as socially equivalent to prostitutes.

12. *guitar*: I.e. a *kithára* (usually translated 'lyre'); very like an East

African *kirar*; a kind of guitar. Like the modern guitar, it was used to accompany songs.

13. *taking up their profession*: See nn. 9, 11. Cf. also Aristotle, *Politics* 1337b: 'To acquire knowledge of liberal arts up to a certain point is not ungentlemanly . . . but to do so for others [i.e. professionally] makes you look rather low-class and slave-like.'

14. *take care of your soul*: Socrates is worried that Protagoras may corrupt Hippocrates' character. This section of the *Protagoras* undermines the accusation that Socrates was himself guilty of 'corrupting the young.'

15. *sophisticated knowledge*: Hippocrates implies that 'sophist' literally means 'a knower (*-istes*) of clever things (*soph-*)'. The word actually derives from the verb *sophízomai*, 'to be clever', 'to be intellectual'.

16. *what does a sophist . . . about?*: Hippocrates means Protagoras is a teacher of rhetoric – the art of speaking – which does not enable people to speak about one particular subject but rather to speak well, whatever the subject may be. Socrates' remark at 334e shows us that he knows this perfectly well.

17. *well or badly*: I.e. having a good life depends on having a good soul (chiefly in the sense of being a good person). The same claim is found at *Apology* 30a, *Crito* 47e, *Republic* 445a, *Meno* 88e, *Gorgias* 477a, 504d. It is a view usually strongly contrasted with hedonism, which Socrates apparently advocates later in this dialogue.

18. *He's busy!*: He means his master, Callias. The grumpy slave at the door is another cliché of Greek comic drama (see, e.g., *Clouds* 133, *Acharnians* 396).

19. *'chorus'*: Perhaps a chorus of initiates, given the reference to Orpheus, the legendary singer and supposed founder of the various Mystery cults. But there is also the suggestion of a comic chorus doing a dance routine. Athenaeus describes this scene as an obvious imitation of comic drama (*Deipnosophistae* 11.115).

20. *And whom next . . . my eyes upon?*: *Odyssey* 11.601. Socrates is comparing their arrival to Odysseus' descent into the underworld. Hippias is described as sitting in judgement, like Minos judging the souls of the dead, while Protagoras, with his band of followers, is like Orpheus and a chorus of initiates, who traditionally frolic around the sunnier parts of Hades (cf. Aristophanes' *Frogs*, 316ff). But why is Callias' house the *underworld*? The combination of allusions to comedy and to the underworld

surely recalls Aristophanes' *Frogs* (in which Dionysus and his slave Xanthias go to the underworld to bring back Euripides). At any rate, the plot of the *Protagoras*, from this point, copies the *Frogs* quite consciously. The second half of the *Frogs* is a contest between the (dead) poets, Aeschylus and Euripides, in which they parody each other's styles to determine who is the better poet and better adviser of the citizens of Athens. Here Plato presents a similar contest between two (dead) philosophers, in which they try out each other's philosophical styles (with much parody from Socrates), similarly to decide which one is the better civic educator. (I speculate that there may be a kind of tribute to Aristophanes in these allusions. The *Frogs* itself was written as an explicit tribute to Euripides, who had just died. The *Protagoras* is reliably dated to the 380s BC; Aristophanes died in 386 BC.)

21. *Tantalus as well!*: *Odyssey* 11.582; continuing the underworld theme. Yet in what follows, Prodicus seems to be presented not as Tantalus but as some kind of strange animal (an underworld monster, perhaps).

22. *sweetheart*: I.e. his *paidiká* ('boy-stuff'). Relationships of this kind were typically between an older man, who played the (traditionally) masculine role of the suitor, and an adolescent, who played a pseudo-feminine role as the object of desire. Pausanias and Agathon (who became a famous tragedian) are depicted as a still devoted couple in the *Symposium* (set about fifteen years later).

23. *Critias, Callaeschrus' son*: This completes the list of the people present. In addition to the sophists, it is an amazing assembly of the Athenian elite. We have Paralus and Xanthippus, sons of Pericles, the most powerful man in Athens; the young Alcibiades (see n. 2); Charmides and Critias (Plato's uncles, who were both involved in the anti-democratic coup of 404 BC); and various other major players. Several of those present have title-roles in Platonic dialogues (Critias, Phaedrus, Alcibiades, Hippias and Charmides) or appear in them. In effect, we have the whole world of Plato in one house. I suspect this continues the underworld theme. There, as here, all the famous people of the past are crammed into the same place at once: see *Apology* 41a–c. Intriguingly, all of the people who make speeches in Plato's *Symposium*, except one, are also present: Socrates, Eryximachus, Phaedrus, Agathon, Pausanias and Alcibiades. The one speaker conspicuously missing is *Aristophanes*.

24. *resentment, and hostility, and ill-will*: People were hostile to sophists because they saw them as innovators in matters of religion, and hence a threat to traditional morality. Protagoras was known as an agnostic, but he seems never to have come to any harm (going by *Meno* 91e).

25. *Homer ... Hesiod ... Simonides*: The claim that these poets were sophists disguised as poets, taken literally, is a tongue-in-cheek absurdity (typical of the sophistic style). But poets were widely regarded as moral educators, and that is how Protagoras sees himself.

26. *Orpheus ... Musaeus*: In the *Phaedo* (69c), Socrates makes a rather similar claim about them – i.e. that the Mystery cults that these mythical singers were connected with, and supposedly founded, were perhaps a form of philosophy in disguise.

27. *Iccus ... Herodicus ... Agathocles ... Pythoclides*: The first two were famous athletic trainers; the other two were music teachers.

28. *for many years*: About twenty-five years, at this point. See *Meno* 91e.

29. *ourselves*: Rather than waiting for slaves to do it for them.

30. *flute*: I.e. an *aulós*, which was a wind instrument, a little like an oboe but double-barrelled, with internal reeds; the same as a modern *mijwiz*.

31. *civic and ethical know-how*: Translates *politiké téchne*, 'citizen's skill/know-how' (*polítes* means 'citizen'; *téchne* means 'skill', 'know-how' or 'craft'); see *Glossary*. It implies (especially in a democratic context) knowing how to contribute to civic decision-making, but also, more simply, knowing how to treat [fellow-] citizens. Plus, Socrates may well intend 'managing one's household' (i.e. looking after one's family) to be part of it. The traditional translation of the same phrase is 'political art' or 'the art of politics'. This is a bit too narrow. Proper treatment of fellow-citizens (e.g. not stealing from them, not killing them) doesn't come under 'the art of politics' in its modern sense, and the traditional phrase now has an inappropriate Machiavellian ring to it.

32. *pretty smart people*: He means that Athenian democratic institutions presumably make sense. This is probably ironic. At any rate, it is not what Plato thinks.

33. *how our city should be run*: Socrates means public ethical questions: whether a given policy, or institution, or public decision, is right or wrong, fair or unfair, good or bad. He does not mean administrative or logistical questions.

34.  *what it is that makes them good*: Translates *areté* (by a para-
     phrase); see *Glossary*.
35.  *his own kind of knowledge*: He means that Pericles was a good
     man and a good citizen, and is making the further assumption
     that those qualities were a form of knowledge or expertise
     (*sophía*). (See *Meno* 93a–94e for a similar but longer discussion.)
36.  *holy cows*: Cows (and various other animals) were sometimes
     deemed sacred to a god and roamed free, sometimes within cities
     or temple precincts.
37.  *guardian*: Alcibiades' father, Clinias, died in battle in 446 BC,
     when Alcibiades was four. Pericles was Alcibiades' and the
     younger Clinias' joint guardian, with Ariphron, his brother.
38.  *you can't make . . . by teaching them*: I.e. 'areté cannot be taught.'
39.  *A long, long time ago*: Protagoras' story (and much of the speech
     that follows it) is presented as an exhibition piece: something
     that he has carefully composed and publicly recited many times.
     The story is written in polished, artificially rhythmic language
     with many unusual turns of phrase. It is not a traditional Greek
     myth. It seems to be an allegorical reworking of (part of) an
     existing rationalist account of the origins of the world. It bears
     a fairly strong resemblance (with some close verbal echoes) to
     such a passage preserved by Diodorus (*Universal History* I, 8)
     and thought by some to be based on a lost work of the materialist
     and humanist philosopher Democritus of Abdera (see Diels and
     Kranz (1985), vol. 2, p. 135), who is reported (perhaps apocry-
     phally) to have been Protagoras' teacher. We know nothing
     certain about that connection or about what exactly Plato was
     drawing from.
40.  *Thinxahead and Thinxtoolate*: In Greek, Prometheus and Epime-
     theus. The names have a deliberate literal sense. Protagoras has
     borrowed these characters, and some of the details, from the
     poet Hesiod (see *Theogonia* 511, *Works and Days* 84).
41.  *scattered here and there*: This probably means as solitary indi-
     viduals, not as scattered groups. Protagoras skirts over the forma-
     tion of families, because he is emphasizing the role of society.
42.  *a sense of right and wrong*: I.e. *díkë* and *aidós*. See *Glossary*.
     This is the crux of the story. Protagoras means that the human
     ethical sense evolved because of the material benefits of co-
     operation and reciprocation (with the implication that it is based
     partly on self-interest, as he states again, more frankly, at 327 b).
     Plato himself rejects this view of the origins of (true) ethical
     understanding: elsewhere he treats it as equivalent to amoralism

(perhaps because it bases morality on nothing 'higher' than our shared material needs). He puts it in the mouth of a nasty hedonist, Callicles, in the *Gorgias* (from 483 a); and it appears as part of a cynical dismissal of morality in the *Republic* (see 358 e). It was also the ethical theory adopted by the later hedonist Epicurus (see his *Principle Doctrines* 31–6).

43. *'Give it out to all of them,' said Zeus*: The top god, in the story, gives us our sense of right and wrong. In fact, this stands for a theory consistent with Protagoras' well-known agnosticism: 'without this widespread sense of right and wrong, people could not have survived; [so it arose naturally].' This may be a social-contract theory (i.e. implying that people consciously agreed to help one another); it also bears a striking resemblance to an evolutionary theory: people who did not have this ethical sense *did not survive*, while those who did, flourished; that's why it exists.

44. *'straightenings'*: I.e. the *euthúnai*. This was the name, in Athens, for public audits that were a check on corruption and inefficiency in political office. *Euthúnein* means 'to straighten'. Protagoras means that this is the punishment for people who don't 'govern . . . according to [the] laws'.

45. *everyone has to be an expert*: More precisely, 'no one is allowed to be an *idiótes* (a non-expert, a layman, an idiot).'

46. *Pherecrates*: A comic playwright. The play referred to is presumably *Hoi Agrioi* (The Wild Ones), which does not survive. It was produced in 421 BC, as far as we know – so this is a slight anachronism.

47. *Eurybatos . . . Phrynondas*: Notorious criminal characters.

48. *aren't a patch on their father*: I.e. not nearly as good as their father at sculpture. By analogy, why should we expect (ethically) good men to have (ethically) good sons?

49. *great expectations*: There is a deliberate sadness in this remark. Paralus and Xanthippus both died just a few years later, during the plague, shortly before Pericles himself (see Plutarch, *Pericles* 36). His death marked the end of Athens' golden age.

50. *having knowledge*: The phrase translates *sophía*; see *Glossary*.

51. *I think it's a thing*: This claim that respect for what's right is a *thing* lets Socrates assign properties to it. Exactly what he means is not totally clear. (He may be punning on the simpler claim: 'I think there is such a thing.') The claim that follows, that 'respect for what's right (*dikaiosúne*) is itself right (*díkaion*)' is probably a fairly ordinary claim (Protagoras apparently thinks so).

*Dikaiosúne* can have a behavioural sense – i.e. it can mean 'doing what's right' – and doing what's right is right. Even taken strictly as referring to a disposition, the term can still self-predicate: '... righteousness – i.e. the state of being righteous – is right, i.e. required of us ethically'; likewise '... being religious (*hosiótes*) is required of us by religion (*hósion*).' This is one among various possible interpretations of a rather unusual passage.

52. *doing what's right*: I.e. *dikaiosúne*. See previous note (and *Glossary*).

53. *Is that what you're saying*: Socrates is questioning the claim that respect for what's right is something different from religiousness. He in effect slides Protagoras' claim that they are 'not like' one another into the less plausible claim that they have nothing in common at all. On the latter view, if doing what's right is right, then being religious must be *not right*. (This is like arguing that anyone who says a car is not like an aeroplane must also think that, since an aeroplane has wheels, a car doesn't have wheels.)

54. *similarity between the two?*: To do what religion requires (i.e. what is *hósion*) in the Greek context means, most prominently, to commit no murder, to look after your parents, to keep your promises, to observe codes of hospitality etc. The overlap with doing what is right is not minor. For a very good discussion of this whole issue, see Plato's *Euthyphro*.

55. *lots of people who think so*: I.e. lots of people think that behaving unethically can get you ahead, and be a 'sensible' (i.e., here, a reasonable or rational) thing to do. For versions of this view, see the amoralism of Thrasymachus in the *Republic* (esp. 343–4), and of Polus (469–71) and Callicles (483–6) in the *Gorgias*. The view that taking advantage of people, if you can get away with it, is a good idea, is also attributed, as here, to 'most people' in the *Republic* (from 358 a). Protagoras is contradicting his speech, in which he spoke highly of ordinary people's ethical sense.

56. *And could we say ... beneficial to people*: The argument is abandoned. Socrates was clearly going to argue that 'good sense' (*sophrosúne*) and 'respect for what's right' (*dikaiosúne*) are much the same thing, probably on the grounds that doing wrong to others is shameful (*aischrón*) and therefore never something you 'do well out of', so never the sensible option; in which case good sense will always make you do what's right – but that's also what respect for what's right does; so they must be the same quality.

57. *I really must be going*: Plato has made sure that we know this is

not true. When Socrates met his friend, right after coming from Protagoras (as described at the start), he mentioned that he had nothing to do.

58. *violation of our nature*: Hippias' little speech is gratuitous, and he comes across as pompous. Yet this distinction – between *law* (or convention) and *nature* – was an important one in the Greek enlightenment. The most interesting application of it is as an *anti-slavery* argument, as follows: 'People are, by nature, created equal, members of the same human family; it is only certain tyrannical laws and social conventions that declare one person free and another a slave, in violation of our common nature.' Aristotle discusses the argument at *Politics* 1253–4. It is perhaps because Plato has no sympathy for it that it appears so obscurely and unflatteringly here (and nowhere else in his works). (See also Popper (2003), chap. 4, esp. p. 72, and p. 374.)

59. *Simonides*: (*c.* 555–470 BC). A famous poet from the island of Ceos; author of songs, including victory odes, dithyrambs and laments; also of epigrams, eulogies and drinking songs. His surviving work displays a down-to-earth generosity and a roughly humanist outlook. This long discussion of a song (after the intervention by the 'chorus' of sophists) works as a literal *choral interlude*, continuing, in my view, the parallels with Greek comedy. (Socrates' pedantic analysis is also highly reminiscent of *Frogs* 1119–1200.) Plato also disagrees with the song very strongly (see nn. 60, 66, 68, 69, 72) on philosophical grounds.

60. *becoming good ... 'bein' good' is hard*: Socrates offers two interpretations (here, and at 343c–345c) of an alleged contrast between these verbs. The verbs are probably not contrasted in the song at all. The emphasis in the Greek is quite wrong for that, and the verb taken as meaning 'to become' (*genésthai*) can also easily mean 'to be'. It's clear (from the several quotations) that Simonides is saying that human beings cannot be perfect (because misfortune will sometimes force us into bad behaviour), and that we should have sympathy for human failings. The contrast between the two quotes, then, may have been something like this: 'It's certainly hard for a [mere] man to be *truly* good – i.e. godlike, *perfect in every way* ... But I don't agree that it's hard to be good; if a man does the best he can, he's good enough in my book.' Socrates is parodying the sophistic style of (pedantic) interpretation. The interpretative claims he makes are, for the most part, deliberately silly. This song only survives in these

quotations, and his garbled reading of it makes its meaning (and even the order of the quoted sections) uncertain.

61. *in Crete and in Sparta*: Contemporary readers knew full well that Cretans and Spartans had no interest whatsoever in philosophy. Socrates' assertion is like claiming that the English rugby team are closet existentialists. As in all good conspiracy theories, Socrates uses the total absence of evidence for his claim as the best reason for believing it.

62. *Thales . . . Chilon . . . group*: These are the 'seven sages'; famous intellectuals, lawmakers and teachers of the seventh and sixth centuries BC.

63. *with the whole of what follows*: Literally, 'as being shifted over'. Socrates (wrongly) wants to take the 'really and truly' (*alathéos*) with the whole sentence, to make it more obviously a response (rather like English '*Actually*, Pittacus . . .'). It is in an unusual position for that, and so needs to be (mentally) 'shifted over' (which is permissible, given the flexibility of word order in Greek).

64. *with the whole sentence*: Literally, 'correctly placed (i.e. taken as if it were) at the end' (see previous note).

65. *to be a good man . . . that's impossible*: Socrates is saying that Simonides is very pedantically disagreeing with the claim that it is *hard* to be good on the grounds that it is not merely hard but impossible (and therefore, strictly speaking, not hard).

66. *and takes him down*: Simonides is saying that desperate situations can force even the best of us into regrettable behaviour. There is a philosophical disagreement here between Plato and Simonides. Plato believes that truly good people remain good in the face of any sort of disaster or emotion, because true ethical knowledge is invincible. (Aristotle attacks the same song on much the same grounds – see *Nicomachean Ethics* 1100b.) This strong disagreement with Simonides' more tragic take on life may explain why Plato chooses this particular song to mangle. (Cf. his all-out attack on tragedy in the *Republic*). As a joke, Socrates ignores the meaning of the lines and reads the Platonic view into them.

67. *any man . . . turns bad*: Socrates is saying that this means 'it's impossible to *be* good,' as if 'to be good' meant 'to be good *all the time*' (which it doesn't).

68. *losing your knowledge*: This is a very *Platonic* sense of 'doing badly'. Simonides means that even decent people may behave badly *when bad things happen to them*; that's what *he* means by

'when he's doing badly'. For Plato, how well you act depends on your knowledge (or lack of it), and in spite of what Socrates says here, his view is probably that *nothing*, in fact, can take away knowledge (see, e.g., 352c and *Meno* 97d), and therefore that *nothing* can make a truly good man act badly.

69. *the ones the gods love*: Simonides means people who are lucky – i.e. being a good person takes luck. Plato doesn't believe this. That may be why Socrates doesn't explain the line.

70. *laying into Pittacus' saying*: Socrates' point is that this passage reinforces the claim that *being* good is impossible (and therefore, pedantically speaking, not hard) by the words 'that which . . . cannot be'. Simonides is in fact saying (much more plausibly) that what is impossible is 'a man completely blame-and-blemish-free'.

71. *the "wilfully . . . my praise"*: Of course, the 'wilfully' *does* go with the 'so long as he . . .' phrase. Socrates assumes, ironically, that Simonides is up to speed with his own famous paradox that 'no one ever does wrong wilfully.'

72. *ain't no shame in it*: In the context, it is clear that Simonides means that when there is no great shame in peoples' mistakes and failures, we should tolerate and accept them; the implication is that people will often fail under extreme pressure, and that there is no great shame in that. This is an idea Plato objects to because of his belief in a kind of ethical knowledge that is invincible. (See 352ff.)

73. *Divers*: Athenians used to put jars of wine and oil into wells in summer, for refrigeration (see, e.g, Aristophanes, *Ecclesiazusae* 1002, *Plutus* 810; Athenaeus, *Deipnosophistae* 3.98). In some cases, 'divers' (presumably household slaves) would have to dive down to the bottom of the wells to deposit and retrieve the jars. This rare sense of the term is recorded in Hesychius' lexicon (*kappa* 3398): 'divers: people who bring up jars from wells'.

74. *People like that are crazy!*: And therefore not brave. In the *Laches*, Plato has Socrates arguing (with obvious reference to this discussion in the *Protagoras*) for the exact opposite view – i.e. that out of those who undertake these (same) dangerous tasks, the ones who have no idea what they are doing obviously have to be much braver than the trained experts.

75. *things that are honourable*: I.e. ethically acceptable things. Protagoras thinks that pursuing pleasure as a unique goal may conflict with ethical considerations (a very reasonable idea). In what follows, Socrates conspicuously ignores this worry. Note that he

makes no mention of 'honourable things' in his reply. 'Good' and 'bad' in his answer are not ethical terms. They just mean 'good for us' and 'bad for us'. Ethical questions appear only much later in the discussion (at 358b; see n.82).

76. *power over other countries, and wealth*: Socrates' list of good things is very unsocratic. In other dialogues he often claims that power and wealth have little value alongside being a good person and having a good soul (see *Meno* 78–80). Recall, though, that at this point he is, by his own admission, filling out what he takes to be the view of 'most people', not his own.

77. *Or are they worth it?*: The line of thought is a little confusing. The example of smoking provides a good illustration: smoking is among 'things that are bad' – i.e. it is, overall, bad for the smoker. Some people smoke, even though they know it's bad for them, 'because they can't resist the pleasure.' But Socrates has shown that the pleasure (that they get out of it) is just some quantity of *good*. So they're now left saying that 'they smoke, knowing that it's bad, because they can't resist what's good [about it].' This is meant to sound absurd, given that the good (that they get out of it) doesn't outweigh the bad, and isn't worth the bad. I.e. the good of smoking is not worth the damage it does to your health.

78. *Obviously . . . wouldn't be making a mistake*: Continuing our illustration: if the 'good things' that came from smoking (the pleasure) outweighed the 'bad things' that came out of it (poor health), then, in choosing to smoke, you *would not be making a mistake* (smoking would not be a mistake). So, if smoking *is* (overall) bad, and *is* a mistake, then the 'good things' that come out of it 'obviously' (i.e. *ex hypothesi*) aren't worth it.

79. *greater amount of bad . . . smaller amount of good!*: E.g. accepting severe illness (greater amount of bad) for the pleasure of smoking (the much smaller amount of good). Socrates is making such a choice sound completely unintelligible by reducing it to a straight, simultaneous and open-eyed exchange, exactly like paying fifty pounds for a ten-pound note.

80. *that obviously . . . pains*: With our example, we started with 'I smoke, which I know is bad for me, because I can't resist the pleasure.' With this second substitution, this becomes 'I smoke, which I know is *painful*, because I can't resist the pleasure.' This sounds absurd. Strictly speaking, it means this: 'I know it's painful (overall), but I can't resist the pleasure (that it gives me now).' So Socrates adds the point that the pleasure does not

outweigh the pain. The pleasures of smoking are obviously not worth the pains (or it would not be painful, or bad, overall).

81. *right or wrong?*: So far Socrates has been filling out a view he attributes to 'most people'; here (with obvious flattery) he gets the sophists to adopt the same (hedonist) view. Note that he still avoids saying that he holds the view himself. He may well do. (His own comment to Protagoras at 333c is perhaps the best approach here: 'I don't care whether you actually believe what you're saying or not. It's the idea itself I want to examine.')

82. *aren't all such actions honourable?*: Socrates has argued that only pleasurable things are *good* (for us), and only painful things *bad* (for us); he has left ethical questions, up to this point, carefully to one side. This claim appears to be a brand new, hedonist take on what should count as 'honourable' i.e. ethical, or ethically acceptable: 'Whatever leads to pleasure we (hedonists) shall deem honourable.'

83. *people who can keep on going*: See 349e.

84. *just a case of ignorance*: I.e. people never do things that they 'believe are frightening' (here, things they think are bad); they only do bad things through not knowing (or thinking) that those things are bad (i.e. not truly fearing them).

85. *we agreed that . . . good for us*: Socrates means the claim he made at 358b: that (1) *all actions that lead to pleasure are honourable* (see n. 82). The claim here, that (2) *all honourable actions are good for us (and hence*, as he adds shortly, *pleasurable)*, is a different claim. This looks like deliberate sleight of hand. Here's the difference: on the earlier (properly hedonist) view, if, e.g., running away is more pleasurable, then running away is to be deemed honourable. By this new claim, since staying and fighting is (traditionally) honourable, it must be pleasurable. The new claim is rather implausible. It is the claim that *any* act of bravery (even, e.g., one that leads to an agonizing death) is pleasurable. Perhaps there are arguments for such a view (Aristotle tries out some at *Nicomachean Ethics* 1169a). But Socrates certainly did not present any in his earlier defence of hedonism. He never showed how traditional honourable actions are supposed to be pleasurable. (He never even mentioned bravery, for instance.)

86. *when they are afraid of something*: He means, for example, that a brave person will be 'afraid of' letting down his friends, or of doing something shameful, or of treating other people wrongly etc. There is no shame in being afraid of that kind of thing.

87. *their lack of fear is shameful*: Cowards aren't afraid of doing

wrong, or of dishonour, or of letting down their friends etc. It is shameful for them not to be afraid of those things. Reckless and crazy people aren't afraid of taking pointless risks, which is also shameful.

88.  *a result of ignorance*: The idea is that *if only they knew* that cowardly actions were in fact more painful, they would act bravely. But what if a coward really and truly *enjoys* being a coward (even enjoys it overall)? It is only in a very strained sense that he 'doesn't know' that cowardice is 'in fact' painful. His failure seems also to lie in a feature of his emotions – in *what he enjoys* – not simply in his intellectual grasp of what is good (and pleasurable). That seems to be strongly implied by the role of pleasure in the account, even if it is denied by Socrates' conclusion. Aristotle makes this point about these claims in the *Protagoras* (see *Nicomachean Ethics* 1144b); and it seems that his overall view (that good people are those who have a grasp of what is good, *and take a corresponding pleasure in* the right things) is strongly influenced by this text in particular.

# MENO

1.  *being good*: I.e. *areté*. See *Glossary*.
2.  *Aristippus*: A Thessalian aristocrat who had political ties with Persia. Xenophon (*Anabasis* 1.1.10, 2.6.28) tells us that Meno led a group of mercenaries, originally lent to Aristippus by Cyrus (the younger brother of Artaxerxes, the Persian King), in Cyrus' failed attempt to overthrow his brother (in 401 BC). Meno was captured, and executed, by Artaxerxes (*Anabasis* 2.6.29). His talk with Socrates takes place just before he left to join Cyrus (he set out in 402 BC, and probably died in 400 BC).
3.  *Gorgias*: (c. 485–380 BC) A famous sophist and teacher of public speaking from Leontini in Sicily. See Plato, *Gorgias*.
4.  *help out your friends and hurt your enemies*: This is the common-sense Greek account of *doing what's right* (of *dikaiosúne*: see *Republic* 332–6). I.e. it is meant to describe ethical behaviour; it is the universal 'tit for tat' ethic: 'treat people well, as long as they treat you well (and punish them when they exploit you).'
5.  *some single form*: Socrates wants to find what it is that all the different cases have in common. This is typical of the 'Socratic method' of ethical inquiry in Plato's earlier dialogues (e.g. *Euthyphro* 5c; *Laches* 191e; *Charmides* 159a; *Republic* I, 331c.)

He is not strictly interested in what absolutely all the uses of the term *areté* have in common. He ignores non-human cases (e.g. 'being a good horse', 'being a good dog') and non-ethical human cases (e.g. 'being a good carpenter'). Perhaps to avoid confusion, no such uses of the term appear anywhere in the *Meno*.

6.  *a matter of . . . other people*: I.e. a good person is one who has what it takes to exercise authority well. Not, in my view, a culturally specific idea. Cf. the quip attributed to Abraham Lincoln: 'Nearly all men can stand adversity, but if you want to test a man's character, give him power.' (Its ancient equivalent, Bias' saying that, 'power will reveal the man', is discussed by Aristotle; see *Nicomachean Ethics*, 1130a.) Of course, Meno's view also flatters the prejudices of the ruling class to which he belongs.

7.  *still be a slave . . . ruling*: He wouldn't be a 'good slave', but why shouldn't he be a good man (who happens to be a slave)? When Diogenes (the Cynic) was being sold as a slave, he was asked if he had any special expertise. 'Yes,' he said, 'I know how to rule people' (Diogenes Laertius, 6.29).

8.  *doing what's right . . . being good*: I.e. *dikaiosúne* is *areté*. See *Glossary*. Meno is expressing a standard Greek view (see, e.g., *Republic* 335c; Aristotle, *Nicomachean Ethics* 1130a). He had also already implied it in his first definition (at 71e).

9.  *The same as being good . . . Or one sort of being good?*: This is neater with the traditional terminology: 'Virtue, or *a* virtue?' The term *areté* can also be used for a particular good quality. The question means: 'Is respect for what's right all there is to being good, or just one good quality among several?'

10. *having knowledge*: I.e. *sophía*; see *Glossary*.

11. *that colour always comes with*: Literally, 'that always follows along with colour'. I.e. whenever there's a colour, there must be a shape – i.e. a shaped object (?) or surface (?) of some kind.

12. *expert quibblers*: Translates *eristikoí*. This refers to sophists and rhetoricians who engaged in devising ingenious arguments for deliberately absurd, or paradoxical, claims as a form of competition or entertainment. Plato's *Euthydemus* provides a vivid illustration of their method. They aim to force people to contradict themselves or to accept absurd conclusions. The general public – inexplicably – tended to confuse 'quibblers' with philosophers.

13. *a more talk-it-through kind of way*: Literally translates the adverb *dialektikóteron*. Socrates is advocating discussion-based

philosophy, the method he always applies to ethical questions. It implies reflecting upon, and building upon, what we already understand. It is therefore also connected in Plato's mind with the acquisition of *a priori* knowledge (knowledge of necessary truths that can be grasped by pure reflection); hence the analogy (in the *Meno*) between mathematics and ethics. I have translated a slightly altered text here (like most editors); see *Appendix*.

14. *Prodicus*: (Active *c.* 440–410 BC); a sophist and (apparently) a friend of Socrates'; the point is that he likes to insist on tiny and pedantic distinctions between words. See *Protagoras* 337, 341.

15. *Empedocles*: (C. 493–433 BC); a philosopher, scientist, poet, statesman and mystic from Akragas in Sicily. His theory of 'outflowings' (*aporrhoaí*) was connected with an explanation of the mechanisms of perception. Epicurus gives us a fairly detailed later version of it (in his *Letter to Herodotus*, 46–53).

16. *a theatrical answer*: In Greek, *tragiké* – i.e. 'tragic' – but in the sense of 'from the stage,' and hence 'bombastic'. Socrates means that the definition contains (in his view) pretentious jargon: 'scientists and their big scary words'. Plato has philosophical objections to mechanistic and scientific explanations (see *Phaedo* 96–9); they are empirical rather than *a priori*, and they do not, in his view, explain *why* things are the way they are.

17. *the Mysteries*: I.e. the Eleusinian Mysteries, a secret religious ceremony connected with the cult of Demeter and Korë (Persephone), held twice a year at Eleusis near Athens. Most Athenians would go to Eleusis during the festivals (a kind of religious pilgrimage) to take part. It offered some sort of spiritual enlightenment. Socrates is comparing that to the effect of doing philosophy. (See also *Phaedo* 69c).

18. *Rejoicing . . . being able*: Line from an unknown song. The poet means that being good is a matter of having a decent character (*rejoicing in* what is 'fair and fine' – i.e. *kalá*: ethical, honourable) and being capable *at such things* – i.e. able to do them. (This is similar to the Aristotelian view of what it is to be good; see, e.g., *Ethics* 1099a, 1179b; *Politics* 1340a). Meno and Socrates (wrongly) take 'fine' to mean simply 'good' – i.e. good for us – or at any rate assume that the one amounts to the other.

19. *loser*: Translates *áthlios*; often translated 'wretched', 'pitiful'.

20. *wanting bad things and then getting them*: The usual view, for Greeks as for us, would be (to adapt the terminology) that to be a loser is a matter of not getting any good things, or of getting lots of very bad things you didn't want. Either might result from

bad luck. Plato's redefinition makes failure in life fully one's own responsibility.

21. *the 'wanting' part applies ... the start*: There is a connection here with the Socratic 'paradox' that being good is simply a matter of knowledge (or that 'virtue is knowledge'). Since we all want the same thing – what's good for us – good people are those who realize or know that ethical actions are good for them.

22. *that's my view exactly!*: In fact, Meno has clearly been brought to this view by Socrates. But being a greedy young man, he's delighted (if a little surprised) by the idea that being good might just be a matter of acquiring things.

23. *gold ... silver ... power ... honour in your city*: It might seem strange that Meno could take such things to be a mark of 'being good' (in any remotely ethical sense). Some commentators think that for Meno (and for many Greeks at the time), 'being a good man' simply meant 'being powerful and successful', with no ethical implication. On the contrary, Plato sees it as a delusion of the powerful that power and status make them *ethically* superior. This is not a specially Greek phenomenon at all. Cf. George Orwell's description of his aristocratic schoolmates: 'Before the [first world] war the worship of money was entirely ... untroubled by any pang of conscience. The goodness of money was as unmistakable as the goodness of health or beauty, and a glittering car, a title, or a horde of servants was mixed up in people's minds with the idea of actual moral virtue' ('Such, Such Were the Joys', in *Shooting an Elephant and Other Essays* (Harmondsworth: Penguin, 2003), p. 329).

24. *the Great King!*: I.e. the Persian King Artaxerxes II (ruled 405–359 BC). He had Meno executed a few years after this conversation (see n. 2). Plato reminds the reader that Meno's greed led to his destruction.

25. *if they don't know ... itself?*: Socrates means that you can't explain something in terms that presuppose the listener already knows what it is. If someone asks, 'What is a jabberwock?' it's no good saying 'A jabberwock is a thing made of jabberwock-parts.' But is that what Meno has done? He has described being good as a disposition made up of respect for what's right, religiousness, bravery etc. – qualities that can quite well be understood independently of the fact that they are 'parts of being good'.

26. *a little while back*: I.e. at 75c–d.

27. *numbfish*: The numbfish (*nárke thalattía*) is a genus of ray (the

electric ray; also called the torpedo). It stuns prey with a powerful
electric charge delivered from special organs in its pectoral fins.
In saying that Socrates also looks just like a numbfish, Meno is
probably referring to his famous snubbed nose (which gives him
a flat face) and perhaps his boggly eyes (see *Theaetetus* 143e,
*Phaedo* 117b; Xenophon, *Symposium* 5.3–8). Numbfish have
very boggly eyes.

28.  *You can't try to find out* . . . : 'Meno's paradox'; a sophistic puzzle
of unknown source. Consider the question 'What is a black hole?'
If you know what a black hole is, why ask? If you don't know
what a black hole is, how do you know what you're asking? This
is discussed again by Plato at *Theaetetus* 165b, and by Aristotle
(*Posterior Analytics* 2.7–10). The version given here by Socrates
is not really the same as Meno's. (See *Introduction*, p. xxi.)

29.  *Pindar*: (C. 518–440 BC). A lyric poet from Boeotia. His surviving songs are delicately written eulogies of athletic champions.
The quotation (from a lost song) that follows deals with the
myth of Persephone, and is connected with Orphism and with
Pythagorean beliefs about reincarnation; note the Pindaric detail
that some good souls will be reincarnated *as athletic champions*.
See Bowra (2000), pp. 89–98.

30.  *the grief, of long ago*: Socrates seems to take this to refer to the
pain caused to others by past crimes. Souls that have paid for
their sins are granted a return to life ('back to the sun-lit world
above'); the implication is that most souls do not return (because
their crimes are too great). Plato's own after-life myths describe
it in rather similar terms (as a place of punishment and reward):
see *Phaedo* 112–14, *Gorgias* 523–7, *Republic* 614–21.

31.  *home-bred*: I.e. born and raised in Meno's household rather than
bought (the same word is used of dogs and domestic birds).

32.  *Tell me then, boy*: 'Boy' (*pai*) is the term of address for a slave
of any age, just as it was used in the US. (Cf. also French *garçon*,
used of a waiter, or English 'maid', used of a domestic worker).
Its use here gave rise to the perception that the slave is a child.
There is no indication of this anywhere in the text. Evidently
Plato doesn't care how old we take the slave to be. His being
a slave guarantees his lack of education in 'liberal arts' like
mathematics.

33.  *what you think*: This phrase uses the impersonal verb *dokeî* (i.e.
'what seems to you [to be the case]'). The point of the remark
becomes clear at 85b (see n. 35).

34.  *he thought he could easily make perfectly good claims*: Socrates

is teasing Meno with a parody of the claim he (Meno) made at 80b. His point is that Meno was as ignorant, and over-confident, about his knowledge of being good as the slave was about the square. To Socrates and Meno, the image of the slave discussing geometry in public is hilarious.

35. *his own opinions*: 'Opinion' translates *dóxa;* this is the noun derived from the impersonal verb *dokeî,* 'it seems'. *Dóxa* is a matter of how things seem to you – i.e. what you think is the case; your opinion, untutored belief, intuition, impression, (rough) idea etc., with obvious application in both mathematics and ethics.

36. *forever*: I.e. 'forever' (*aeí*) in the sense of for all time, since all eternity. 'At some point' then means at some point since the beginning of time. The words could also easily mean 'Either he acquired it at some point during his life, or he's always had it – i.e. since his birth.' But Socrates seems to be saying, 'Either (a) the slave had acquired this (now latent) knowledge at some point since the beginning of time, or (b) he had had it for all of time.' On that reading, on option (b), his soul existed before his birth: and that inference is crucial to the argument. (See also n. 37.)

37. *during the life he's living now*: I.e. even if he got his bits of latent knowledge since the beginning of time, his soul still must have existed before his birth, because he didn't get them in his present life. There is also the possibility that he acquired them at birth rather than either before birth or 'in the life he's living now'. That possibility is not considered here. In the *Phaedo* (76c), when Plato reworks this argument, he considers and dismisses it.

38. *you prefer to be 'free'*: A sarcastic dig at the ideal of freedom (a democratic notion: see, e.g., Thucydides, 2.37.2; Aristotle, *Politics,* 1317 a40). Plato implies that 'freedom', for Meno, is really just a lack of self-control. On this view, (politically) free people are often 'slaves' to their desires and delusions (so political freedom, for them, has no value). See *Gorgias* 491d and *Republic* 576a.

39. *on a hypothesis*: Literally, 'on an under-laying'; an assumption. Socrates wants something they can 'lay under' – i.e. take for granted – that will make their question (whether being good can be taught) more manageable.

40. *If the area is such that . . . done to it*: The example illustrates the role of a *hypothesis* very clearly, but the details are baffling. For various explanations, see Bluck (1964), pp. 441–61, or Sharples (1985), pp. 158–60. The question is whether an area can be

inscribed as a triangle in a given circle. 'Its given line' is usually taken (awkwardly) to refer to the diameter of the circle, and 'matching' may mean either 'identical in area to' or 'having the same proportions as'. Socrates' example may of course just be a mimicking of geometrical language without making sense. 'If blah-de-blah, then dum-de-dum' makes the point perfectly well.

41. *a good thing*: I.e. in a non-ethical sense: good for us, in the way that we might say that health and strength are 'good things'. For Socrates this can be taken for granted. It is a fundamental premise of Platonic ethics that being good is always in your own best interests. Elsewhere (especially *Republic* 335–66, 608–14 and *Gorgias* 483–92), Socrates has to argue for this view; here it is assumed (i.e. is a *hypothesis*).

42. *in the general sphere of knowledge*: I.e. itself a form of knowledge or somehow connected with knowledge, but not in the sense of merely being knowable.

43. *if we are good, we do good*: I.e. if we are *agathoí* (good), then we are *ophélimoi* (people who do good). See *Glossary*.

44. *all good things do us good, don't they?*: Two different claims in one: (1) that good *things* must do us some kind of good, and (2) that good *people* do good to those around them (a kind of utilitarian view).

45. *features of the soul*: I.e. in this context, qualities of mind and character – 'internal good things' – as opposed to the 'external good things' just discussed.

46. *a sort of fearlessness . . . a kind of wisdom*: For this idea of bravery as mere fearlessness, see *Laches* 193a, where Socrates suggests that foolish fearlessness – e.g. taking on a vastly superior army – is especially brave. Plato more often treats bravery as having ethical and prudential implications (see, e.g., *Protagoras* 359–60, where Socrates insists that you can't be both brave and stupid). 'Wisdom' translates *phrónesis* – i.e. practical understanding (embracing our grasp of what is good and bad, right and wrong). So the practical/ethical implications of our term *wisdom* are appropriate. Throughout the dialogue, Plato apparently uses the word interchangeably with both *epistéme* (knowledge) and *sophía* (knowledge, expertise, cleverness) and *nous* (sense, understanding), even though it is his distinctive view, rather than obvious, that these are all the same thing. Aristotle, for one (see *Nicomachean Ethics* 6.7, 6.12) strongly disagrees with the view that *phrónesis* is the same as knowledge.

47. *our having a good life*: I.e. *eudaimonía*.

48. *in and of themselves*: Here, 'good in themselves' means unconditionally good – i.e. always good, no matter what. Plato is
straining to set these goods apart from knowledge. But by Plato's
own view, is knowledge unconditionally good? Plato asks
'What's the good of money, if you don't know how to use it?'
But, likewise, what's the good of knowing how to use it if you
don't have any?

49. *a kind of wisdom ... entirely or partly*: This seems the easiest
way to take the phrase (considered in itself). Some interpreters
take the line like this: 'Being good is wisdom; either all of wisdom
or part of wisdom.' Then, either way, it is nothing but wisdom,
making it *fully* teachable. (Because if it were not fully teachable,
then perhaps that rather messes up the argument.) That may
be right. But note that a good man's bravery was analysed as
*fearlessness plus wisdom*; and there was the implication of *self-
control plus wisdom* and *generosity plus wisdom*, and so on
(88a–b). So being good, there at least, was not *just* wisdom. In
the *Republic*, Plato claims that the soul of a good man is part
wisdom and part traits of character (see 442–4).

50. *it can't be ... naturally good*: I.e. because wisdom (equated by
Plato with knowledge) does not come naturally; it has to be
taught, or acquired through philosophy.

51. *just as we do with public gold*: The Athenians used the west
section of the Parthenon, on the Acropolis, as a treasury. This
remark seems to allude to the plan Plato endorsed in the *Republic*
(see bks 3–7) of setting aside genetically superior children (with
'natures of gold') and training them up to be the elite rulers of
the state.

52. *Anytus*: (Active *c.* 415–390 BC). An Athenian politician, patriotic
and conservative, who played a major role in the restoration of
the democracy, with Thrasybulus, in 403 BC, after the rule of
the Thirty Tyrants. At this time he was one of the most important
politicians in Athens. It is implied that he is Meno's host. Most
importantly, he was one of the men who, in 399 BC, prosecuted
Socrates for impiety and for 'corrupting the young'.

53. *Polycrates' bribe*: Ismenias was a Theban democratic political
leader. Plato appears to be taking a swipe at him. There is no
satisfactory explanation of who Polycrates is. My own guess is
that the name should in fact be *Timo*crates. Ismenias allegedly
took a large bribe from Timocrates, an agent of a Persian general,
Tithraustes, as payment for stirring up trouble between Thebes
and Sparta (Xenophon, *Hellenica* 3.5.1, 5.2.35; *Hellenica*

*Oxyrhynchia* 7.2). (This took place in 395 BC; by Plato's rather rough chronology that seems fine.)

54. *brains and diligence*: Socrates is describing Anthemion as a self-made man, someone who has acquired his own wealth as a businessman and then entered the political domain (Xenophon implies that he and Anytus were leather-tanners: *Apology* 29.1). This sounds like praise but his comments are probably ironic. At any rate, *Plato* has no respect for men of this kind. A measure of his disdain is the fact that in his ideal state (described in the *Republic*), this kind of social mobility – the rise of a man of trade into political responsibility – is declared the greatest possible crime against the state (see 434a–d).

55. *the great Athenian public*: Ironic. For Plato, the election of men like Anytus to public office (he was, at least, elected *strategós* in 409 BC) demonstrates the folly of democracy.

56. *a shocking suggestion*: Anytus has a typical anti-intellectual view of sophists and philosophers. Men of his type equated intellectual innovation with perversity, and scientific curiosity with religious scepticism and ethical relativism. That is why he feels that sophists are 'depraved' (see 91c). Aristophanes' *Clouds* provides easily the best picture of this sort of attitude.

57. *Phidias*: (Active 465–425 BC). He was responsible, notably, for the huge gold and ivory statues of Athena in the Parthenon and of Zeus at Olympia, and for the design of the Parthenon frieze.

58. *or a local*: Anytus is hinting, with some menace, that Socrates himself may be a 'local' sophist.

59. *family friend*: The implication is that, at the very least, Anytus' father, Anthemion, had some kind of guest-friendship (*xenía*) with Meno's father or grandfather.

60. *decent*: Translates *kalós k'agathós* ('fine-and-good'), a phrase that (often) has class connotations as well as ethical ones (rather like English 'gentleman'); but Anytus here seems to be speaking of Athenian men in general. This view is the same as the one Plato attributes to Meletus, another of Socrates' prosecutors, in the *Apology* (24–5); see also *Protagoras* 323–8. It is the democratic view: if plenty of Athenians are 'decent men', it makes sense that there should be broad access to the political process.

61. *Themistocles*: (C. 524–459 BC); most famous for developing Athenian naval power and leading Athens in the face of the Persian invasion of 480 BC.

62. *lacking natural ability*: Plato seems to be thinking of the boy's

'nature' very broadly: he means 'he wasn't congenitally incapable of learning things.'

63. *Aristides*: (Active *c*. 495–467 BC); a contemporary and rival of Themistocles; nicknamed 'the Righteous'. Socrates names him at *Gorgias* 526b as a man who was not corrupted by power. He commanded the Athenian forces at the battle of Plataea in 480 BC and had a hand in the setting up of the Delian League.

64. *Lysimachus*: He appears in Plato's *Laches* (179c), where he complains that his father both spoiled and neglected him, and that that's why he never amounted to much.

65. *Thucydides*: (C. 500–420 BC). Not the historian (though perhaps his uncle); a prominent conservative politician and rival of Pericles.

66. *allies*: I.e. the city-states of the Aegean that were allied with Athens (and, later, governed by Athens) after the Persian wars.

67. *watch your back*: This is a threat. There is also dramatic irony. The reader knows that this is a man who later had Socrates put to death.

68. *what it . . . means to 'badmouth' a man*: Perhaps an allusion by Plato to later events, as with Anytus' last remark. A very late source (Diogenes Laertius, 2.43) says that the Athenians regretted executing Socrates and sent Anytus into exile. There may be something in the story. Plato refers indirectly, with some bitterness, to their swift change of heart (*Crito* 48c5); and Xenophon confirms Anytus' posthumous bad name (*Apology* 35). So Plato, writing fifteen to twenty years later, has Socrates saying to Anytus: 'You think that's bad? You have no idea. Wait till you find out what people are going to say about *you*.' Note that the *Meno* itself fulfils the prophecy pretty well. For a different interpretation, see Bluck (1964), p. 338, and Sharples (1985) p. 178.

69. *That's what most impresses me about Gorgias*: In the *Gorgias* there is a discussion of this point (455b–461b). Gorgias claims, at one point, that as you shouldn't blame a boxing-coach if one of his athletes uses his skills to beat up his own father, likewise you shouldn't blame a teacher of public speaking if one of his pupils uses his speaking skills unethically (456d–457b). I.e. it is not the business of the teacher of rhetoric to make people good.

70. *Theognis*: (Active *c*. 550 BC); a writer of elegiacs – i.e. songs written in couplets – from Megara; his surviving work contains much friendly advice of this kind.

71. *people who claim to teach it*: I.e. sophists (or rather, some of them).

72. *bad at the ... thing they claim to teach*. I.e. *bad at being good*, i.e. simply bad (in an ethical sense). He means that sophists are considered immoral by people like Anytus.

73. *and in my case, Prodicus*: In the *Protagoras* Socrates similarly claims that he is Prodicus' student, but the context suggests friendly sarcasm (339–41). Elsewhere he says he once went to one of his one-drachma (i.e. bargain) lectures (*Cratylus* 384b).

74. *We were right to agree ... weren't we?*: I.e. at 87e.

75. *'show us the way'*: Socrates and Meno did not exactly agree that good people do good by 'showing [others] the way'. What was agreed (at 88d–89a) was that for an individual person's life to go well, *wisdom* has to be 'showing [*that person*] the way'. This (perhaps unconscious) shift suggests an analogy in Plato's mind between the two – i.e. an analogy (developed in the *Republic*) between good rulers directing the other citizens and parts of the soul directing the rest of the soul.

76. *Daedalus' statues*: Daedalus was a legendary sculptor, architect, inventor and craftsman of magical ability. His sculptures were said to have been so life-like that they actually came alive.

77. *by figuring out what makes them true*: Aitías logísmo(i); literally (?) 'by a figuring out of a cause'. 'A cause' (*aitía*) may mean here an explanation of why they are true – i.e. a justification, or perhaps 'what causes them to be the case'. See *Republic* 473c–484a for Plato's later and more detailed discussion of this difference between 'opinions' and philosophically grounded knowledge. There is also an example of unstable ethical 'opinions' in his *Euthyphro*. There Euthyphro complains that his ideas (about religion) won't 'stay put', and compares Socrates to Daedalus, for making them move about (11b–d).

78. *the next thing we asked*: At this point Socrates begins a recapitulation of the discussion from 89c–96c.

79. *fortune-tellers and soothsayers*: Plato probably sees 'fortune-tellers and soothsayers' as charlatans (see *Euthyphro* 1–5 and *Republic* 364c), and this remark may be meant as a veiled insult. The point is that the ethical and political views of these ordinary 'good men' are unphilosophical and therefore inadequate. See *Republic* 473c–484a.

80. *'That man's inzpired'*: Most editors think that Plato here imitated the Spartan dialect (writing not *theíos*, which we have in the manuscripts, but *seíos*).

81.  *We'll talk with him again*: Perhaps this can be taken by the reader
     to refer, by dramatic irony, to Socrates' trial.
82.  *unless, that is, there were a man*: I.e. such a man would disprove
     the theory that being good cannot be taught and suggest that it
     is a kind of knowledge after all. Plato may be referring, cryp-
     tically, to Socrates himself (a man who, by his 'talk-it-through'
     method, is genuinely able to make people good); or to himself,
     future author of the *Republic* and would-be educator of phil-
     osopher-statesmen.
83.  *He alone . . . in the world below*: Odyssey 10.495.
84.  *you may well be doing Athens a favour*: Plato (not Socrates)
     means, if Meno (or anyone) could have 'calmed Anytus down',
     then he might not have prosecuted Socrates, which would have
     been the greatest possible favour to Athens.

# PENGUIN CLASSICS

## THE ODYSSEY HOMER

'I long to reach my home and see the day of my return. It is my never-failing wish'

The epic tale of Odysseus and his ten-year journey home after the Trojan War forms one of the earliest and greatest works of Western literature. Confronted by natural and supernatural threats – shipwrecks, battles, monsters and the implacable enmity of the sea-god Poseidon – Odysseus must test his bravery and native cunning to the full if he is to reach his homeland safely and overcome the obstacles that, even there, await him.

E. V. Rieu's translation of *The Odyssey* was the very first Penguin Classic to be published, and has itself achieved classic status. For this edition, his text has been sensitively revised and a new introduction added to complement E. V. Rieu's original introduction.

'One of the world's most vital tales ... *The Odyssey* remains central to literature' Malcolm Bradbury

Translated by E. V. Rieu
Revised translation by D. C. H. Rieu, with an introduction by Peter Jones

# PENGUIN CLASSICS

### THE ILIAD   HOMER

'Look at me. I am the son of a great man. A goddess was my mother. Yet death and inexorable destiny are waiting for me'

One of the foremost achievements in Western literature, Homer's *Iliad* tells the story of the darkest episode in the Trojan War. At its centre is Achilles, the greatest warrior-champion of the Greeks, and his refusal to fight after being humiliated by his leader Agamemnon. But when the Trojan Hector kills Achilles's close friend Patroclus, he storms back into battle to take revenge – although knowing this will ensure his own early death. Interwoven with this tragic sequence of events are powerfully moving descriptions of the ebb and flow of battle, of the domestic world inside Troy's besieged city of Ilium, and of the conflicts between the gods on Olympus as they argue over the fate of mortals.

E. V. Rieu's acclaimed translation of Homer's *Iliad* was one of the first titles published in Penguin Classics, and now has classic status itself. For this edition, Rieu's text has been revised, and a new introduction and notes by Peter Jones complement the original introduction.

Translated by E. V. Rieu
Revised and updated by Peter Jones with D. C. H. Rieu
Edited with an introduction and notes by Peter Jones

# PENGUIN CLASSICS

## THE POLITICS   ARISTOTLE

'Man is by nature a political animal'

In *The Politics* Aristotle addresses the questions that lie at the heart of political science. How should society be ordered to ensure the happiness of the individual? Which forms of government are best and how should they be maintained? By analysing a range of city constitutions – oligarchies, democracies and tyrannies – he seeks to establish the strengths and weaknesses of each system to decide which are the most effective, in theory and in practice. A hugely significant work, which has influenced thinkers as diverse as Aquinas and Machiavelli, *The Politics* remains an outstanding commentary on fundamental political issues and concerns, and provides fascinating insights into the workings and attitudes of the Greek city-state.

The introductions by T. A. Sinclair and Trevor J. Saunders discuss the influence of *The Politics* on philosophers, its modern relevance and Aristotle's political beliefs. This edition contains Greek and English glossaries, and a bibliography for further reading.

Translated by T. A. Sinclair
Revised and re-presented by Trevor J. Saunders

# PENGUIN CLASSICS

---

## THE REPUBLIC   PLATO

'We are concerned with the most important of issues, the choice between a good and an evil life'

Plato's *Republic* is widely acknowledged as the cornerstone of Western philosophy. Presented in the form of a dialogue between Socrates and three different interlocutors, it is an inquiry into the notion of a perfect community and the ideal individual within it. During the conversation other questions are raised: what is goodness?; what is reality?; what is knowledge? *The Republic* also addresses the purpose of education and the roles of both women and men as 'guardians' of the people. With remarkable lucidity and deft use of allegory, Plato arrives at a depiction of a state bound by harmony and ruled by 'philosopher kings'.

Desmond Lee's translation of *The Republic* has come to be regarded as a classic in its own right. His introduction discusses contextual themes such as Plato's disillusionment with Athenian politics and the trial of Socrates. This new edition also features a revised bibliography.

Translated with an introduction by Desmond Lee

---

# THE STORY OF PENGUIN CLASSICS

**Before 1946** ...'Classics' are mainly the domain of academics and students, without readable editions for everyone else. This all changes when a little-known classicist, E. V. Rieu, presents Penguin founder Allen Lane with the translation of Homer's *Odyssey* that he has been working on and reading to his wife Nelly in his spare time.

**1946** *The Odyssey* becomes the first Penguin Classic published, and promptly sells three million copies. Suddenly, classic books are no longer for the privileged few.

**1950s** Rieu, now series editor, turns to professional writers for the best modern, readable translations, including Dorothy L. Sayers's *Inferno* and Robert Graves's *The Twelve Caesars*, which revives the salacious original.

**1960s** The Classics are given the distinctive black jackets that have remained a constant throughout the series's various looks. Rieu retires in 1964, hailing the Penguin Classics list as 'the greatest educative force of the 20th century'.

**1970s** A new generation of translators arrives to swell the Penguin Classics ranks, and the list grows to encompass more philosophy, religion, science, history and politics.

**1980s** The Penguin American Library joins the Classics stable, with titles such as *The Last of the Mohicans* safeguarded. Penguin Classics now offers the most comprehensive library of world literature available.

**1990s** The launch of Penguin Audiobooks brings the classics to a listening audience for the first time, and in 1999 the launch of the Penguin Classics website takes them online to a larger global readership than ever before.

**The 21st Century** Penguin Classics are rejacketed for the first time in nearly twenty years. This world famous series now consists of more than 1300 titles, making the widest range of the best books ever written available to millions – and constantly redefining the meaning of what makes a 'classic'.

The Odyssey continues ...

*The best books ever written*

PENGUIN (🐧) CLASSICS

SINCE 1946

Find out more at www.penguinclassics.com